Also by Vivian Gornick

The Odd Woman
and the City

The Odd Woman and the City

A MEMOIR

Vivian Gornick

Farrar, Straus and Giroux   New York

Farrar, Straus and Giroux
18 West 18th Street, New York 10011

Printed in the United States of America
First edition, 2015

Portions of this book originally appeared, in somewhat different
form, in *The New Yorker*, *The Paris Review*, *Poetry*, and *The
Threepenny Review*.

Owing to limitations of space, all acknowledgments for permission
to reprint previously published material can be found on page 177.

Library of Congress Cataloging-in-Publication Data
Gornick, Vivian.
    The odd woman and the city : a memoir / Vivian Gornick. —
1st Edition.
        pages   cm
    ISBN 978-0-374-29860-9 (hardback) — ISBN 978-0-374-71168-9
(e-book)
    1. Friendship.   2. Love.   3. City and town life—New York
(State)—New York.   I. Title.

BF575.F66 G676 2015
818'.5403—dc23

                                                    2014039376

Designed by Jonathan D. Lippincott

Farrar, Straus and Giroux books may be purchased for educational,
business, or promotional use. For information on bulk purchases,
please contact the Macmillan Corporate and Premium Sales
Department at 1-800-221-7945, extension 5442, or write to
specialmarkets@macmillan.com.

www.fsgbooks.com
www.twitter.com/fsgbooks • www.facebook.com/fsgbooks

10   9   8   7   6   5   4   3   2   1

Author's Note

Reader beware: All names and identifying characteristics have been changed. Certain events have been reordered and some characters and scenes are composites.

The Odd Woman
and the City

Leonard and I are having coffee at a restaurant in midtown.

"So," I begin. "How does your life feel to you these days?"

"Like a chicken bone stuck in my craw," he says. "I can't swallow it and I can't cough it up. Right now I'm trying to just not choke on it."

My friend Leonard is a witty, intelligent gay man, sophisticated about his own unhappiness. The sophistication is energizing. Once, a group of us read George Kennan's memoir and met to discuss the book.

"A civilized and poetic man," said one.

"A cold warrior riddled with nostalgia," said another.

"Weak passions, strong ambitions, and a continual sense of himself in the world," said a third.

"This is the man who has humiliated me my entire life," said Leonard.

Leonard's take on Kennan renewed in me the thrill of revisionist history—the domesticated drama of seeing the world each day anew through the eyes of the aggrieved—and reminded me of why we are friends.

We share the politics of damage, Leonard and I. An impassioned sense of having been born into preordained social inequity burns brightly in each of us. Our subject is the unlived life. The question for each of us: Would we have manufactured the inequity had one not been there, ready-made—he is gay, I am the Odd Woman—for our grievances to make use of? To this question our friendship is devoted. The question, in fact, defines the friendship—gives it its character and its idiom—and has shed more light on the mysterious nature of ordinary human relations than has any other intimacy I have known.

For more than twenty years now Leonard and I have met once a week for a walk, dinner, and a movie, either in his neighborhood or mine. Except for the two hours in the movie, we hardly ever do anything else but talk. One of us is always saying, Let's get tickets for a play, a concert, a reading, but neither of us ever seems able to arrange an evening in advance of the time we are to meet. The fact is, ours is the most satisfying conversation either of us has, and we can't bear to give it up even for one week. It's the way we feel about ourselves when we are talking that draws us so strongly to each other. I once had my picture taken by two photographers on the same day. Each likeness was me, definitely me, but to my eyes the face in one photograph looked broken and faceted, the one in the other of a piece. It's the same with me and Leonard. The self-image each of us projects to the other is the one we carry around in our heads: the one that makes us feel coherent.

Why, then, one might ask, do we not meet more often than once a week, take in more of the world together, extend each other the comfort of the daily chat? The problem is, we both have a penchant for the negative. Whatever the circumstance, for each of us the glass is perpetually half-empty. Either he is registering loss, failure, defeat—or I am. We cannot help ourselves. We would like it to be otherwise, but it is the way life feels to each of us: and the way life feels is inevitably the way life is lived.

One night at a party I fell into a disagreement with a friend of ours who is famous for his debating skills. At first, I responded nervously to his every challenge, but soon I found my sea legs and then I stood my ground more successfully than he did. People crowded round me. That was wonderful, they said, wonderful. I turned eagerly to Leonard. "You were nervous," he said.

Another time, I went to Florence with my niece.

How was it? Leonard asked. "The city was lovely," I said, "my niece is great. You know, it's hard to be with someone twenty-four hours a day for eight days, but we traveled well together, walked miles along the Arno, that river is beautiful." "That *is* sad," Leonard said. "That you found it irritating to be so much with your niece."

A third time I went to the beach for the weekend. It rained one day, was sunny another. Again, Leonard asked how it had been. "Refreshing," I said. "The rain didn't daunt you," he said.

I remind myself of what *my* voice can sound like. My voice, forever edged in judgment, that also never stops registering the flaw, the absence, the incompleteness. My voice that so often causes Leonard's eyes to flicker and his mouth to tighten.

At the end of an evening together, one or the other of us will impulsively suggest that we meet again during the week, but only rarely does the impulse live long enough to be acted upon. We mean it, of course, when we are saying goodbye—want nothing more than to renew the contact immediately—but going up in the elevator to my apartment, I start to feel on my skin the sensory effect of an evening full of irony and negative judgment. Nothing serious, just surface damage—a thousand tiny pinpricks dotting arms, neck, chest—but somewhere within me, in a place I cannot even name, I begin to shrink from the prospect of feeling it again soon.

A day passes. Then another. I must call Leonard, I say to myself, but repeatedly the hand about to reach for the phone fails to move. He, of course, must be feeling the same, as he doesn't call either. The un-acted-upon impulse accumulates into a failure of nerve. Failure of nerve hardens into ennui. When the cycle of mixed feeling, failed nerve, and paralyzed will has run its course, the longing to meet again acquires urgency, and the hand reaching for the phone will complete the action. Leonard and I consider ourselves intimates because our cycle takes only a week to complete.

•

Yesterday, I came out of the supermarket at the end of my block and, from the side of my eye, registered the beggar who regularly occupies the space in front of the store: a small white guy with a hand perpetually outstretched and a face full of broken blood vessels. "I need something to eat," he was whining as usual, "that's all I want, something to eat, anything you can spare, just something to eat." As I passed him I heard a voice directly behind me say, "Here, bro. You want something to eat? Here's something to eat." I turned back and saw a short black man with cold eyes standing in front of the beggar, a slice of pizza in his outstretched hand. "Aw, man," the beggar pleaded, "you know what I . . ." The man's voice went as cold as his eyes. "You say you want something to eat. Here's something to eat," he repeated. "I bought this for you. *Eat it!*" The beggar recoiled visibly. The man standing in front of him turned away and, in a motion of deep disgust, threw the pizza into a wastebasket.

When I got to my building I couldn't help stopping to tell Jose, the doorman—I had to tell *someone*—what had just happened. Jose's eyes widened. When I finished he said, "Oh, Miss Gornick, I know just what y'mean. My father once gave me such a slap for exactly the same thing." Now it was my eyes that widened. "We was at a ball game, and a bum asked me for something to eat. So I bought a hot dog and gave it to him. My dad, he whacked me across the face. 'If you're gonna do a thing,' he said, 'do it right. You don't buy someone a hot dog without you also buying him a soda!' "

•

In 1938, when he was just months from dying, Thomas Wolfe wrote to Maxwell Perkins, "I had this 'hunch,' and wanted to write you and tell you . . . I shall always think of you and feel about you the way it was that Fourth of July three years ago when you met me at the boat, and we went out to the cafe on the river and had a drink and after went on top of the tall building, and all the strangeness and the glory and the power of life and of the city was below."

The city, of course, was New York—the city of Whitman and Crane—that fabled context for the creation myth of the young man of genius arriving in the world capital, as in a secular tableau of annunciation, with the city waiting for him and him alone to cross the bridge, stride the boulevard, climb to the top of the tallest building, where he will at last be recognized for the heroic figure he knows himself to be.

Not my city at all. Mine is the city of the melancholy Brits—Dickens, Gissing, Johnson, especially Johnson—the one in which we are none of us going anywhere, we're there already, we, the eternal groundlings who wander these mean and marvelous streets in search of a self reflected back in the eye of the stranger.

In the 1740s, Samuel Johnson walked the streets of London to cure himself of chronic depression. The London that Johnson walked was a city of pestilence: open sewers, disease, poverty; destitution; lit by smoking torches; men cutting each other's throats in deserted alleys at midnight. It was of this city that Johnson said, "When a man is tired of London, he is tired of life."

For Johnson the city was always the means of coming up from down under, the place that received his profound discomfort, his monumental unease. The street pulled him out of morose isolation, reunited him with humanity, revived in him his native generosity, gave him back the warmth of his own intellect. On the street Johnson made his enduring observations; here he found his wisdom. Late at night, when he went prowling for tavern conversation, he experienced the relief of seeing his own need mirrored in the company he found: those who drank and talked of Man and God till the light broke because none of them wanted to go home either.

Johnson hated and feared village life. The closed, silent streets threw him into despair. In the village his reflected presence was missing. Loneliness became unbearable. The meaning of the city was that it made the loneliness bearable.

•

I have always lived in New York, but a good part of my life I longed for the city the way someone in a small town would, yearning to arrive at the capital. Growing up in the Bronx was like growing up in a village. From earliest adolescence I knew there was nter-of-the-world, and that I was far from it. e same time, I also knew it was only a subway ride away, downtown in Manhattan. Manhattan was Araby.

At fourteen I began taking that subway ride, walking the length and breadth of the island late in winter, deep in summer. The only difference between me and someone like me from Kansas was that in Kansas one makes the immigrant's lonely leap once and forever, whereas I made many small trips into the city, going home repeatedly for comfort and reassurance, dullness and delay, before attempting the main chance. Down Broadway, up Lexington, across Fifty-Seventh Street, from river to river, through Greenwich Village, Chelsea, the Lower East Side, plunging down to Wall Street, climbing up to Columbia. I walked these streets for years, excited and expectant, going home each night to the Bronx, where I waited for life to begin.

The way I saw it, the West Side was one long rectangle of apartment houses filled with artists and intellectuals; this richness, mirrored on the East Side by money and social standing, made the city glamorous, and painfully exciting. I could taste in my mouth world, sheer world. All I had to do was get old enough and New York would be mine.

As children, my friends and I would roam the streets of the neighborhood, advancing out as we got older, section by section, until we were little girls trekking across the Bronx as though on a mission to

the interior. We used the streets the way children
growing up in the country use fields and rivers,
mountains and caves: to place ourselves on the map
of our world. We walked by the hour. By the time
we were twelve we knew instantly when the speech
or appearance of anyone coming toward us was the
slightest bit off. If a man approached and said,
"How ya doin', girls? You girls live around here?"
we knew. If a woman wasn't walking purposefully
toward the shopping street, we knew. We knew also
that it excited us to know. When something odd
happened—and it didn't take much for us to consider something odd, our sense of the norm was
strict—we analyzed it for hours afterward.

A high school friend introduced me to the streets
of upper Manhattan. Here, so many languages and
such striking peculiarities in appearance—men in
beards, women in black and silver. These were people I could see weren't working-class, but what class
were they? And then there was the hawking in
the street! In the Bronx a lone fruit and vegetable
man might call out, "Missus! Fresh tomatoes today!" But here, people on the sidewalk were selling
watches, radios, books, jewelry—in loud, insistent
voices. Not only that, but the men and women passing by got into it with them: "How long'll that
watch work? Till I get to the end of the block?" "I
know the guy who wrote that book, it isn't worth a

dollar." "Where'd ya get that radio? The cops'll be at my door in the morning, right?" So much stir and animation! People who were strangers talking at one another, making one another laugh, cry out, crinkle up with pleasure, flash with anger. It was the boldness of gesture and expression everywhere that so captivated us: the stylish flirtation, the savvy exchange, people sparking witty, exuberant responses in one another, in themselves.

In college, another friend walked me down West End Avenue. I'd never seen a street as wide and stately as this one, with doormen standing in front of apartment houses of imposing height that lined the avenue for a mile and a half. My friend told me that in these great stone buildings lived musicians and writers, scientists and émigrés, dancers and philosophers. Very soon no trip downtown was complete without a walk on West End from 107th Street to Seventy-Second. For me, the avenue became emblematic. To live here would mean I had arrived. I was a bit confused about whether I'd be the resident artist/intellectual or be married to him—I couldn't actually see myself signing the lease—but no matter; one way or another, I'd be in the apartment.

In summer we went to the concerts at Lewisohn Stadium, the great amphitheater on the City College campus. It was here that I heard Mozart and Beethoven and Brahms for the first time. These

concerts came to an end in the mid-sixties, but in
the late fifties, sitting on those stone bleacher seats
July after July, August after August, I knew, I just
knew, that the men and women all around me lived
on West End Avenue. As the orchestra tuned up and
the lights dimmed in the soft, starry night, I could feel
the whole intelligent audience moving forward as
one, yearning toward the music, toward themselves
in the music: as though the concert were an open-air
extension of the context of their lives. And I, just
as intelligently I hoped, leaned forward, too, but I
knew that I was only mimicking the movement. I'd
not yet earned the right to love the music as they
did. Within a few years I began to see it was entirely
possible that I never would.

As I saw myself moving ever farther toward the
social margin, nothing healed me of a sore and angry heart like a walk through the city. To see in the
street the fifty different ways people struggle to remain human—the variety and inventiveness of survival techniques—was to feel the pressure relieved,
the overflow draining off. I felt in my nerve endings
the common refusal to go under. That refusal became company. I was never less alone than alone in
the crowded street. Here, I found, I *could* imagine
myself. Here, I thought, I am buying time. What a
notion: buying time. It was one I shared with Leonard for years.

I grew up and moved downtown but sure enough, nothing turned out as expected. I went to school but the degree did not get me an office in midtown. I married an artist but we lived on the Lower East Side. I began to write but nobody read me above Fourteenth Street. For me, the doors to the golden company did not open. The glittering enterprise remained at a distance.

•

Among my friends, I am known for my indifference to acquisition. People make fun of me because I seem to want nothing; neither do I know the name of anything, nor can I readily differentiate between the fake and the genuine, the classy and the mediocre. It isn't high-minded disinterest, it is rather that things have always sent me into a panic; a peasant-like discomfort with color, texture, abundance— glamour, fun, playfulness—is the cause of my unease. All my life I've made do with less because "stuff" makes me anxious.

Leonard has developed a style of living that seems the direct obverse of my own, but, truth to tell, I think it the mirror image. Overflowing with Japanese prints, Indian rugs, eighteenth-century furniture upholstered in velvet, his place feels like a set of museum rooms of which he is the curator. I see that he is filling in the physical surround as desperately as I am not. Yet he's never been at home in his apartment any more than I am in mine; he, too, needs to feel concrete beneath his feet.

•

After I graduated from college, New York meant Manhattan, but for Leonard, who'd also grown up in the Bronx, it remained the neighborhoods. From the time I first knew him—more than thirty years ago now—he walked the streets as I never had, into Brooklyn, Queens, Staten Island. He knew Sunnyside, Greenpoint, Red Hook; Washington Heights, East Harlem, the South Bronx. He knew the meaning of a shopping street in Queens with half the stores boarded up, a piece of Brooklyn waterfront restored, a garden lot in Harlem full of deranged-looking flowers, a warehouse on the East River converted to a Third World mall. He knew which housing projects worked and which were a devastation. And it wasn't just the streets he knew. He knew the piers, the railroad yards, the subway lines. He had Central Park and Prospect Park by heart. He knew the footbridges on the East River; the ferries, the tunnels, the beltways. He knew Snug Harbor and City Island and Jamaica Bay.

He often reminded me of the street-urchin protagonists in postwar Italian movies: those handsome, ragged children of Rossellini's who imprint on Rome by knowing the city inside out. Leonard always looked like that to me when we took one of our long hikes through the boroughs: hungry, as only a working-class kid can be, for information; the kind of information that makes the ground beneath your feet yours. With him as my guide, the neighborhoods spread out for miles in all directions, often looking to my uninformed eye like wasteland until I began to see them as Leonard did: an incomparable sea of ghettos forever bleeding new life into a rectangle of glamour and prosperity.

On these treks of ours, the character of time-and-space often changed as we walked. The concept of "hours" evaporated. The streets became one long ribbon of open road stretched out before us, with nothing to impede our progress. Time expanded to resemble time in one's childhood, when it seemed never to end, as opposed to time now: always scarce, always pressing, always a fleeting marker of one's emotional well-being.

•

At a New Year's party, Jim comes rushing toward me. Sarah nods and turns away. A year ago I was tight with one, two years ago with the other. To-night I realize I haven't seen him in three months, her in six. A woman who lives three blocks from me appears, her eyes shimmering. "I miss you!" she

breathes wistfully, as though we're lovers in war-
time separated by forces beyond our control. Yes, I
nod, and move on. We'll embrace happily, me and
all these people: not a glance of grievance, not a syl-
lable of reproach among us. And, indeed, there is
no call for grievance. Like pieces in a kaleidoscope
that's been shaken, we've all simply shifted position
in the pattern of intimate exchange. Many of us
who not so long ago were seeing one another regularly will meet now more often by accident than by
design: in a restaurant, on the bus, at a loft wedding. Ah, but here's someone I haven't seen in years.
Suddenly, a flare of intensity and we're meeting
once a week for the next six months.

I am often reminded of the tenement friendships in my childhood, circumstantial one and all.
Round, dark-eyed women, filled with muted understanding for the needs of the moment. What difference did it make if the next-door neighbor was
called Ida or Goldie when you needed someone to
lend you ten bucks or recommend an abortionist or
nod her head during an outburst of marital rage?
It mattered only that there was a next-door neighbor.
These attachments, as Sartre might have put it, were
contingent rather than essential.

As for us: Never before in history has so much
educated intelligence been expended on the idea of
the irreplaceable—the essential—self; and never be-

fore has aversion to the slightest amount of psychological discomfort allowed so many to be treated as the contingent other.

•

The third-century Roman writer Caius understood that his many difficulties with friendship began with an inability to make peace with himself. "No man has a right to expect friendship from others," he wrote, "who is not a friend to himself. This is the first great duty of mankind, to be friends to themselves. There are thousands who are not only hostile to themselves, but who thwart the best intentions of others to serve them, and yet they are the persons from whom may be heard the loudest complaints that 'there is no such thing as a friend in the world!'"

•

Samuel Taylor Coleridge worshipped a definition of friendship that embodied an ideal that could be traced back to Aristotle. Living at a time when persons of sensibility yearned for communion of the spirit, Coleridge suffered from its frequent failure to materialize in friendship; but the pain did not threaten his faith, not even when he lost the friendship that defined all others.

Coleridge and William Wordsworth met in 1795

when they were, respectively, twenty-three and twenty-five years old. Wordsworth—grave, thin-skinned, self-protective—was, even then, steadied by an inner conviction of his own coming greatness as a poet; Coleridge, on the other hand—brilliant, explosive, self-doubting to the point of instability—was already into opium. Anyone except them could see that they were bound to come a cropper. In 1795, however, a new world, a new poetry, a new way of being, was forming itself, and at that moment, both Wordsworth and Coleridge, each feeling the newness at work in himself, saw proof of its existence reflected in the person of the other.

The infatuation lasted a little more than a year and a half. At the end of that time, the chaos within Coleridge doubled its dominion; the pride in Wordsworth stiffened into near immobility. The person each had been for nearly two years—the one who had basked in the unbroken delight of the other—was no more. It wasn't exactly that they were returned to the persons they had been before; it was only that never again would either feel his own best self in the presence of the other.

One's own best self. For centuries, this was the key concept behind any essential definition of friendship: that one's friend is a virtuous being who speaks to the virtue in oneself. How foreign is such a concept to the children of the therapeutic culture!

Today we do not look to see, much less affirm, our best selves in one another. To the contrary, it is the openness with which we admit to our emotional incapacities—the fear, the anger, the humiliation—that excites contemporary bonds of friendship. Nothing draws us closer to one another than the degree to which we face our deepest shame openly in one another's company. Coleridge and Wordsworth dreaded such self-exposure; we adore it. What we want is to feel *known*, warts and all: the more warts the better. It is the great illusion of our culture that what we confess to is who we are.

•

Every night when I turn the lights out in my sixteenth-floor living room before I go to bed, I experience a shock of pleasure as I see the banks of lighted windows rising to the sky, crowding round me, and feel myself embraced by the anonymous ingathering of city dwellers. This swarm of human hives, also hanging anchored in space, is the New York design offering generic connection. The pleasure it gives soothes beyond all explanation.

•

The phone rings. It's Leonard.

"What are you doing?" he asks.

"Reading Krista K," I reply.

"Who's she?" he asks.

"Who's she!" I say. "She's one of the most famous writers in Eastern Europe."

"Oh," he says matter-of-factly. "What's the book like?"

"A bit claustrophobic." I sigh. "You don't really know where you are most of the time, or who's speaking. Then every twenty pages or so she says, 'Ran into G this morning. Asked him how long he thought we could go on like this. He shrugged. Yes, I said.'"

"Oh," Leonard says. "One of those. Bor-ring."

"Tell me," I say, "don't you ever mind sounding like a Philistine?"

"The Philistines were a much maligned people," he says. "Have you seen Lorenzo lately?"

"No, why?"

"He's drinking again."

"For God's sake! What's wrong now?"

"What's wrong *now*? What's right now? What's ever right for Lorenzo?"

"Can't you talk to him? You know him so well."

"I *do* talk to him. He nods along with me as I speak. I know, I know, he says, you're right, I've got to pull it together, thanks so much for saying this, I'm so grateful, I don't know why I fuck up, I just don't know."

"Why *does* he fuck up?"

"Why? Because if he's not fucking up he doesn't know who he is."

Leonard's voice has become charged.

"It's unbelievable," he swears on, "the muddle in his mind. I say to him, What do you want, what is it you *want*?"

"Tell me," I cut in, "what do *you* want?"

"Touché." Leonard laughs drily.

There follows a few long seconds of vital silence.

"In my life," he says, "I have known only what I *don't* want. I've always had a thorn in my side, and I've always thought, When this thorn is removed I'll think about what I want. But then that particular thorn would be removed, and I'd be left feeling emptied out. In a short time another thorn would be inserted into my side. Then, once again, all I had to think about was being free of the thorn in my side. I've never had time to think about what I *want*."

"Maybe somewhere in there is a clue to why Lorenzo drinks."

"It's disgusting," Leonard says softly. "To be this old and have so little information. Now, *there's* something Krista K could write about that would interest me. The only problem is she thinks information is what the KGB was after."

.

In the drugstore I run into ninety-year-old Vera, a Trotskyist from way back who lives in a fourth-floor walk-up in my neighborhood and whose voice is always pitched at the level of soapbox urgency. She is waiting for a prescription to be filled, and as I haven't seen her in a long while, on impulse I offer to wait with her. We sit down in two of the three chairs lined up near the prescription counter, me in the middle, Vera on my left, and on my right a pleasant-looking man reading a book.

"Still living in the same place?" I ask.

"Where'm I gonna go?" she says, loudly enough for a man on the pickup line to turn in our direction. "But y'know, dolling? The stairs keep me strong."

"And your husband? How's he taking the stairs?"

"Oh, him," she says. "He died."

"I'm so sorry," I murmur.

Her hand pushes away the air.

"It wasn't a good marriage," she announces. Three people on the line turn around. "But, y'know? In the end it doesn't really matter."

I nod my head. I understand. The apartment is empty.

"One thing I gotta say," she goes on, "he was a no-good husband, but he was a great lover."

I can feel a slight jolt in the body of the man sitting beside me.

"Well, that's certainly important," I say.

"Boy, was it ever! I met him in Detroit during the Second World War. We were organizing. In those days, everybody slept with everybody, so I did, too. But you wouldn't believe it . . ." And here she lowers her voice dramatically, as though she has a secret of some importance to relate. "Most of the guys I slept with? They were no good in bed. I mean, they were bad, really *bad*."

Now I feel the man on my right stifling a laugh.

"So when you found a good one"—Vera shrugs—"you held on to him."

"I know just what you mean," I say.

"Do you, dolling?"

"Of course I do."

"You mean they're still bad?"

"Listen to us," I say. "Two old women talking about lousy lovers."

This time the man beside me laughs out loud. I turn and take a good long look at him.

"We're sleeping with the same guys, right?" I say.

Yes, he nods. "And with the same ratio of satisfaction."

For a split second the three of us look at one another, and then, all at once, we begin to howl. When the howling stops, we are all beaming. Together

we have performed, and separately we have been
received.

•

No one is more surprised than me that I turned out
to be who I am. Take love, for instance. I had always
assumed that, in this regard, I was like every other
girl of my generation. While motherhood and marriage had never held my interest, and daydreaming
myself on some revolutionary barricade was peculiar among my classmates, I always knew that one
day Prince Passion would come along, and when he
did, life would assume its ultimate shape: *ultimate*
being the operative word. As it happened, a number
of PP look-alikes did appear, but there was no ultimate anything. Before I was thirty-five I had been as
much bedded as any of my friends, and I had also
been twice married, twice divorced. Each marriage
lasted two and a half years, and each was under-
taken by a woman I didn't know (me) to a man I
also didn't know (the figure on the wedding cake).

It was only after these marriages were over that
I matured sexually—that is, I became conscious of
myself as a person preoccupied with desiring rather
than being desired; and *that* development gave me
an education. I learned that I was sensual but not a
sensualist; that I blissed out on orgasm but the earth
didn't move; that I could be strung out on erotic ob-

session for six months or so but was always waiting for the nervous excitement to die down. In a word: Lovemaking was sublime, but it wasn't where I lived. And then I learned something more.

In my late thirties I had an affair with a man I cared for and who cared for me. This man and I were both drawn to the energy of mind and spirit that each of us felt in the other. But for this man, too—intelligent, educated, politically passionate as he was—the exercise of his sexual will was central to any connection he made with a woman. There was not a moment when we were together that he wasn't touching me. He never walked into my house that his hand wasn't immediately on my breast; never embraced me that he wasn't reaching for my genitals; never lay beside me that he wasn't trying to make me come. When, after we'd been together some months, I began to object to what had started to feel like an on-automatic practice, he would invariably put his arms around me, nuzzle my neck, and whisper in my ear, "C'mon, you know you like it." As I did genuinely love him and he me—we had memorable times together—I would stare at him at such moments, shake my head in exasperation, but then let it go.

One day he suggested that I let him sodomize me, something we'd not done before. I demurred. Next day he made the same suggestion. Again, I demurred.

"How do you know you won't like it," he persisted, "if you've never done it?" He wore me down: I agreed to try it once. No, no, he said, I must agree to do it three times and *then* if I said no it would be no. So we did it three times, and truth to tell, I didn't hate the physical sensation as much as I had thought I would—almost against my will, my body responded—but I definitely did not like it.

"Okay," I said, "I've done it three times, and I don't want to do it anymore."

We were lying in bed. He nuzzled my neck and whispered in my ear, "C'mon. Just one more time. You know you like it."

I drew away then and looked directly into his face. "No," I said, and was startled by the finality in my own voice.

"What an unnatural woman you are!" he exploded at me. "You know you want to do it. *I* know you want to do it. Yet you fight it. Or is it me you're fighting?"

Once again, I stared at him: only this stare was different from those other stares. A man was pressing me to do something I did not want to do, and pressing me in a manner he would never have applied to another man: by telling me that I didn't know what I wanted. I felt my eyes narrowing and my heart going cold. For the first—but not the last—time, I consciously felt men to be members of a species separate from myself. Separate and foreign. It was as though an invisible membrane had fallen between me and my lover, one fine enough to be penetrated by desire but opaque enough to obscure human fellowship. The person on the other side of the membrane seemed as unreal to me as I felt myself to be to him. At that moment I didn't care if I never again got into bed with a man.

I did of course get into bed with them—love, quarrel, and bliss out many more times after this man and I parted—but the memory of that fine, invisible separation haunted me; and more often than I like to remember, I saw it glistening as I gazed into the face of a man who loved me but was not persuaded that I needed what he needed to feel like a human being.

In time, I came to know other women who would have analyzed the experience differently but immediately understood what I was talking about when I described the invisible curtain. It comes with the territory, most of them said, shrugging. They had made their peace with an arrangement that was as it had ever been. I saw that I could not. For me, it had become the pea beneath the twenty mattresses: an irritation of the soul that I could not accommodate.

Work, I said to myself, work. If I worked, I thought, pressing myself against my newly hardened heart, I'd be a person in the world. What would it matter then that I was giving up "love"?

As it turned out, it mattered more than I had ever dreamed it would. As the years went on, I saw that romantic love was injected like dye into the nervous system of my emotions, laced through the entire fabric of longing, fantasy, and sentiment. It haunted the psyche, was an ache in the bones; so deeply embedded in the makeup of the spirit, it hurt the eyes to look directly into its influence. It would be a cause of pain and conflict for the rest of my life. I prize my hardened heart—I have prized it all these years—but the loss of romantic love can still tear at it.

•

A wooden barrier has been erected on my street around two squares of pavement whose concrete has been newly poured. Beside the barrier is a single wooden plank laid out for pedestrians, and beside that, a flimsy railing. On an icy morning in midwinter I am about to grasp the railing and pull myself along the plank when, at the other end, a man appears, attempting the same negotiation. This man is tall, painfully thin, and fearfully old. Instinctively, I lean in far enough to hold out my hand to him. Instinctively, he grasps it. Neither of us speaks a word until he is safely across the plank, standing beside me. "Thank you," he says. "Thank you very much." A thrill runs through me. "You're welcome," I say, in a tone that I hope is as plain as his. We each then go our separate ways, but I feel that "thank you" running through my veins all the rest of the day.

It was his voice that had done it. That voice! Strong, vibrant, self-possessed: it did not know it belonged to an old man. There was in it not a hint of that beseeching tone one hears so often in the voice of an old person when small courtesies are shown—"You're so kind, so kind, so very kind," when all you're doing is hailing a cab or helping to unload a shopping cart—as though the person is apologizing for the room he or she is taking up in the world. This man realized that I had not been inordinately helpful; and he need not be inordinately thankful. He was recalling for both of us the ordinary recognition that every person in trouble has a right to expect, and every witness an obligation to extend. I had held out my hand, he had taken it. For thirty seconds we had stood together—he not pleading, I not patronizing—the mask of old age slipped from his face, the mask of vigor dropped from mine. In the midst of American dysfunction, global brutality, and personal defensiveness, we had, each of us, simply come into full view, one of the other.

•

Leonard has a friend, Tom, who is a great collector
of parables. For Tom, the mere act of waking in the
morning is a source of apprehension; the parables
comfort and refresh him. The other day Leonard repeated two of Tom's newest to me. In the first, "A
woman falls off an ocean liner. Hours later, she is
missed. The crew turns the ship around. They go
back and they find her because she's still swimming."
In the second, "A man decides to kill himself, jumps
off a high bridge, changes his mind in midair, shapes
his body into a dive, and survives." Life is hell, the
species is doomed, but ya gotta keep swimming.

"Why do you think in the first story the protagonist is a woman, in the second a man?" I asked
Leonard.

"But the man is gay, dummy!" he replied. "The
woman has fallen off the boat, she hasn't jumped,
and she'll be damned if an accident is going to do
her in; she starts swimming *immediately*. The man,
on the other hand, is all suicidal indecisiveness. He's
more than halfway into his plunge before he decides
it's better to live than to die. Gay, definitely."

•

There are two categories of friendship: those in
which people enliven one another and those in which

people must be enlivened to be with one another. In the first category one clears the decks to be together; in the second one looks for an empty space in the schedule.

I used to think this distinction more a matter of one-on-one relationships than I now do. These days I look upon it more as a matter of temperament. That is, there are people who are temperamentally inclined to be enlivened, and others for whom it is work. Those who are inclined are eager to feel expressive; those for whom it's work are more receptive to melancholia.

New York friendships are an education in the struggle between devotion to the melancholy and attraction to the expressive. The pavements are filled with those longing to escape the prison sentence of the one into the promise of the other. There are times when the city seems to reel beneath its impact.

•

A few weeks ago a woman who lives on my floor invited me to a Sunday brunch. This woman has taught grade school for years, but she looks upon teaching as a day job. In *real* life, she says, she is an actor. None of the people at the brunch—all in their forties and fifties—knew one another well, and some didn't know the others at all, but it soon became clear that everyone at the table also thought of the work they did as day jobs; every one of them saw him- or herself as having a vocation in the arts, albeit one without material achievement. The chatter on that Sunday morning was animated by one account after another of this or that failed audition or publication or gallery showing, each one ending with "I didn't prepare hard enough," or "I knew I should have rewritten the beginning," or "I don't send out enough slides." What was striking was the sympathy that each self-reproach called to life in the others. "Oh, you're too hard on yourself!" was heard more than once. Then, abruptly, looking directly at the last person to say "You're too hard on yourself," a woman who'd been silent started to speak.

"When I got divorced," she said, "I had to sell the house in Westchester. A couple in the business of importing Chinese furniture and art objects bought the house and began moving things in a week before I was to leave. One night I went down into the basement and began looking through some of their crates. I found a pair of beautiful porcelain vases. On impulse, I took one. I thought, They've got everything, I've got nothing, why shouldn't I? When I moved, I took the vase with me. A week later the husband called and said this funny thing had happened, one of this pair of vases had disappeared, did I know anything about it. No, I said, sounding as bemused as he, I didn't know anything about it, I'd never even seen the vases. I felt awful then. But I didn't know what to do. I put the vase in a closet and never looked at it again. Ten years passed. Then I began thinking about the vase. Soon the thought of the vase began to obsess me. Finally, this past year I couldn't stand it anymore. I packed up the vase as carefully as I could, and sent it back to them. And I wrote a separate letter, saying I didn't know what had possessed me, why I had taken this thing that belonged to them, and I wasn't asking for forgiveness, but here it was back. A few weeks later the wife called me. She said she'd gotten this strange letter from me, she didn't know what I was talking about, and then this package came, and inside the package was about a thousand shards of something or other. What on earth was it that I had taken and was now sending back?"

•

Leonard and I are sitting in his living room, me in the tall gray velvet chair, he on the brown canvas couch.

"The other day," I tell him, "I was accused of being judgmental. What a laugh, I thought. You should have known me ten years ago. But you know?

I'm *tired* of apologizing for being judgmental. Why *shouldn't* I be judgmental? I *like* being judgmental. Judgmental is reassuring. Absolutes. Certainties. How I have loved them! I want them back again. Can't I have them back again?"

Leonard laughs and drums his fingers restlessly along the wooden armrest of his beautiful couch.

"Everyone used to seem so grown up," I say. "Nobody does anymore. Look at us. Forty, fifty years ago we would have been our parents. Who are we now?"

Leonard gets up and crosses the room to a closed cabinet, opens it, and takes out a torn package of cigarettes. My eyes follow him in surprise. "What are you doing," I say, "you've stopped smoking." He shrugs and extracts a cigarette from the package.

"They passed," Leonard says, "that's all. Fifty years ago you entered a closet marked 'marriage.' In the closet was a double set of clothes, so stiff they could stand up by themselves. A woman stepped into a dress called 'wife' and the man stepped into a suit called 'husband.' And that was it. They disappeared inside the clothes. Today, we don't pass. We're standing here naked. That's all."

He strikes a match and holds it to his cigarette.

"I'm not the right person for this life," I say.

"Who is?" he says, exhaling in my direction.

•

At ten in the morning, two old women are walking ahead of me on West Twenty-Third Street, one wearing a pink nylon sweater, the other a blue. "Did you hear?" the woman in pink says. "The pope appealed to capitalism to be kind to the poor of the world." The woman in blue responds, "What did capitalism say?" As we're crossing Seventh Avenue, the woman in pink shrugs. "So far it's quiet."

At noon, a man at a grocery counter stands peering at the change in his hand. "You gave me $8.06," he says to the young woman behind the cash register. "I don't think that's right." She looks at the coins and says, "You're right. It shoulda been $8.60," and gives the man the correct change. He continues to stare at his open palm. "You put the six and the zero in the wrong place," he says. "It shoulda been the other way around." Now it's the woman who stares. When at last the man turns away, I shake my head sympathetically. "What I put up with all day long," she says with a sigh as I pile my purchases on the counter. "Would you believe this? A guy comes up to the counter with an item. It's marked wrong. I can see right away, it's the wrong amount. I tell him, 'Listen, that's the wrong price. Believe me, I know the prices, I been working in the store two years.' He says to me, 'That's nothing to be proud of,' and he marches out."

At three in the afternoon, a distinguished-looking couple is standing under the awning of the posh Regency Hotel on Park Avenue. The man has iron-gray hair and regular features and is wearing an expensive overcoat. The woman is alcoholic thin, has blond, marcelled hair, and is wearing mink. She looks up at him as I pass them, and her face lights up. "It's been a *wonderful* afternoon," she says. The man embraces her warmly and nods directly into her face. The scene excites my own gratitude: how delicious to see people of the moneyed classes acting with simple humanity! Later I run into Sarah, a tired socialist of my acquaintance, and I tell her about the couple on Park Avenue. She listens with her customary Marxist moroseness and says, "You think she knows from a wonderful afternoon?"

•

In the 1940s, Charles Reznikoff, a New York poet, walked the streets of his native city. Reznikoff was not a solitary—he was married, worked at a government agency, had literary friends—but the lucidity in his work comes from an inner silence so keen, so luminous, the reader cannot help feeling that he wandered because he needed some reminder of his own humanity that only the street could provide:

I was walking along Forty-Second Street as
     night was falling.
On the other side of the street was Bryant
     Park.
Walking behind me were two men
and I could hear some of their conversation:
"What you must do," one of them was
     saying to his companion,
"is to decide on what you want to do
"and then stick to it. Stick to it!
"And you are sure to succeed finally."

I turned to look at the speaker giving such
     good advice
and was not surprised to see that he was old.
But his companion
to whom the advice was given so earnestly,
was just as old;
and just then the great clock on top of a
     building across the park
began to shine.

Time and again the drama of human beings
sighting each other across the isolation unfolds for
Reznikoff in the street:

During the Second World War, I was going
     home one night

along a street I seldom used. All the stores
    were closed
except one—a small fruit store.
An old Italian was inside to wait on
    customers.
As I was paying him I saw that he was sad.
"You are sad," I said to him. "What is
    troubling you?"
"Yes," he said, "I am sad." Then he added
in the same monotone, not looking at me:
"My son left for the front today and I'll
    never see him again."
"Don't say that!" I said. "Of course you
    will!"
"No," he answered. "I'll never see him
    again."

Afterwards, when the war was over,
I found myself once more in that street
and again it was late at night, dark and
    lonely;
and again I saw the old man alone in the
    store.
I bought some apples and looked closely at
    him:
his thin wrinkled face was grim
but not particularly sad. "How about your
    son?" I said.

"Did he come back from the war?" "Yes,"
   he answered.
"He was not wounded?" "No. He is all right."
"That's fine," I said. "Fine!"
He took the bag of apples from my hands
   and groping inside
took out one that had begun to rot
and put in a good one instead.
"He came back at Christmas," he added.
"How wonderful! That was wonderful!"
"Yes," he said gently, "it was wonderful."
He took the bag of apples from my hands
   again
and took out one of the smaller apples and
   put in a large one.

I often wonder what Reznikoff's poems would
sound like were he walking the streets today.

•

"Every man alone is sincere," said Ralph Waldo
Emerson. "At the entrance of a second person, hy-
pocrisy begins . . . A friend, therefore, is a sort of
paradox in nature."

•

I had an affair with a downtown playwright. Two
things about this man: He was an ex-alcoholic, and

he was phobic about leaving the city. I was too old
to think him poetic, but I did. He promised to remain sober, and he kept that promise. He promised
to be faithful, but he didn't keep that one. After he
left me I suffered, in equal part, heartbreak and
outrage. "You're leaving *me*?" I wailed. "I'm sup-
posed to leave *you*!"

An alcoholic, Leonard shrugged.

An ex-alcoholic, I explained.

I don't care what kind of alcoholic, Leonard said.

Now, we're walking up Sixth Avenue in midtown and suddenly—I don't know why, maybe I'm
remembering the playwright—I recall a wonderful
line of Frank O'Hara's that I saw threaded in letters
of steel along the marina balustrade in Battery Park
City. "One need never leave the confines of New
York to get all the greenery one wishes," O'Hara
had written. "I can't even enjoy a blade of grass un-
less I know there's a subway handy, or a record store
or some other sign that people don't totally regret
life." I repeat the line to Leonard, whose eyes crinkle
up with pleasure. "An overpraised poet," he says,
"but sometimes he was really quite marvelous."

"Yes," I say, nodding. I can feel O'Hara's sentence repeating itself in my head, and I'm starting
to yearn toward it.

"It's a pity," Leonard says, "that—"

"He died so young," I break in. Leonard stares at me.

"His only bi-og-raphy was so shal-low . . ."

"Oh!"

"*Hon*-estly." He peers at me. "Can't have a serious conversation with you anymore."

"Okay, okay." I pull myself together. "Yes, he does deserve a good biography."

"Not so much for himself," Leonard says. "He was a mad bad boy all his life, who knows what the work would have come to, but his life was a sign of the times. It was one of those moments [the fifties] when aesthetics replaced politics, and you know gays are always welcome then. It was the end of the war, New York was at its loveliest, a few men were feeling bold enough, and unafraid enough, to be themselves openly. If you had a sense of privilege, as O'Hara did, you could push the thing to unheard-of limits. Which he did. And because he did, because he was so astonishingly bold and *got away with it*, things began to change."

As we're passing Radio City Music Hall, Leonard looks up at the garish old movie palace. "You had to have beauty and class and Ivy League self-confidence," he says, "all of which O'Hara had. It would have been unthinkable for someone like me to try it."

With these words he falls into a reverie whose rue is palpable.

I nudge him. "But if O'Hara hadn't lived it out then, you would not be walking here with me now." I laugh. "Even *I* would not be walking here with me now."

He joins me in the laugh: grudgingly. He hates giving up his grievances. He equates them with the irony he says saved his life. *That* he will never give up.

In the evening we have dinner at the home of a pair of psychoanalysts we both know only slightly. The people at the table are homophobic, worshipful of "values," and avid to talk culture. The dinner is expensive, but the conversation is junk food. The analysts address themselves exclusively to me. I feel trapped. Repeatedly, I turn to Leonard to enjoy myself, but I am alone at the table. He has withdrawn into a remoteness I cannot penetrate. Later we walk through the dark and silent streets. The night is cold. We burrow into ourselves. After a time Leonard says to me, "I don't interest them. And the part of me that's interesting frightens them."

We do not draw closer because of what he has just said—I've been alone in his presence too many hours now—but life feels easier to bear for the clarity his words have imposed on an otherwise pointless evening.

My friendship with Leonard began with me invoking the laws of love: the ones that involve expectancy. "We are one," I decided shortly after we met. "You are me, I am you, it is our obligation to save each other." It took years for me to realize this sentiment was off the mark. What we are, in fact, is a pair of solitary travelers slogging through the country of our lives, meeting up from time to time at the outer limit to give each other border reports.

•

The front door of my building is just a few steps from a subway entrance. Between the two a man stands, begging. He's been standing here almost every day now for more than two years. His name is Arthur. He is black, in his thirties, handsome, neatly dressed. He holds a paper cup in his hand and in a warm, patient voice intones over and over again, "Ladies and gentlemen, I wonder if you can help me out. I don' have anywhere to sleep, and I'd sure like a little food in my stomach. I don' drink, take drugs, or do any criminal activities. All I'm askin' for is your support in these hard times. Anything you can spare will be appreciated."

I hardly ever give Arthur money—as a child of the Left I remain categorically opposed to begging—but I talk to anyone who talks to me. Arthur and I chat every morning. (How ya doin'? Okay, and you?

Not bad, not bad. Don't stay out too long, it's gonna be cold today.) Sometimes if I'm in a hurry, all I do is wave hello. Invariably, he'll then rag me. "Lookin' good ta-day," he'll call out, "real good." I'll start to laugh and his voice will follow me, continuing to call out in that tender, baiting way he has.

The other day a man came up out of the subway just as I was walking through my front door. Arthur held out his cup. The man jerked his body away from Arthur's hand as though from something diseased, on his face a look of murderous disgust. Arthur went on droning as though nothing out of the way had occurred, but I felt ill. "What is this all *about*?" I cried. "Are you going to do this for the rest of your *life*?"

His laughing eyes looked down at me. I was a mark like any other. "Ma'am," he said, and went into his routine, "I look for a job, the Man he don' wanna help me, he does everything he can to keep me down, he don' care if I starve in the street."

Arthur is smart and he has words, but so do I. I stood there arguing with him. Then, in the middle of a sentence, he said sharply, "I'll decide when the vacation is over."

I stared at him. I don't know what he saw in my face, but his own softened perceptibly. Very quietly he said, "It doesn't mean what it meant when you were young."

•

Once, in the late seventies, when I was on my high horse for radical feminism, I was invited to give the commencement address at a small women's college. I called my mother to let her know that this honor had been bestowed on me.

"You were asked to deliver a *commencement* address?" she exclaimed incredulously.

"Yes," I said.

"You mean someone writes the speech and you give it?"

"No," I said, "I write the speech and I give it."

"Tell me," she said the next day, "how come they asked *you*. I mean how is it exactly that they ask someone like you."

"*Ma!*" I said.

And the day after that: "Do you have to show the speech to them before you give it?" she asked. "I mean, a dean or someone, he'll see what you're going to say?"

"No . . ." I sighed. "I don't have to show it to anyone."

Her eyes rested silently on my face.

"*Nu,*" she said at last, "if they don't like what you say all they'll do is tell you to go home."

Meaning: After all, it *is* America, they can't kill you.

•

I learned early that life was either Chekhovian or
Shakespearean. In our house there was no contest.
My mother lay on a couch, in a half-darkened room,
one arm flung across her forehead, the other pressed
against her breast. "I'm lonely!" she cried, and from
every quarter of the tenement, women, and men
also, flapped about, trying to assuage an anguish of
the soul they took to be superior. But she turned
away, her eyes closed in frantic dissatisfaction. She
wanted a solace of the spirit none of them could
provide. They were not the right people. No one
around her was the right person. There had been
only one right person, and now he was dead.

She had elevated love to the status of the holy
grail. To find love was not simply to have sexual
happiness, it was to achieve a place in the universe.
When she married my father, she told me, a cloud
of obscurity lifted from her soul. That's how she
put it: a cloud of obscurity. Papa was magic: his
look, his touch, his understanding. She leaned
forward when she got to the end of this sentence.
Understanding was the talismanic word. Without
understanding, she said, she didn't know she was
alive; with understanding, she felt centered and in
the world. In my father's presence she responded
with a depth she hadn't known she possessed to

poetry, politics, music, sex: everything. She closed her eyes dramatically. *Everything*. When he died, she said, "everything" went with him. The cloud over her soul returned, blacker than ever: now it blotted out the earth.

The depression was profound and, apparently, nonnegotiable, persisting undiminished and undiluted for years on end. She could not forget the absolute *rightness* of what had once been hers. Whatever was now being offered, it would not do. Nothing was ever again exactly the right thing, no one exactly the right one. Refusal of the approximate took on a life of its own.

I became my mother's daughter. Very young, I was not able to find myself interesting without intelligent response. I required the company of minds attuned to my own, but no one around gave me back the words I needed to hear. I was forever telling the children on the block a story that had grown out of something that had just happened at school, in the grocery store, in the tenement building where I lived. I'd give them the narration, then I'd sum up, giving them the sentence that delivered the meaning of the story. After that I wanted someone to speak a sentence that would let me know my own had been received. Instead, eager looks evaporated, expressions turned puzzled or hostile, and, inevitably, someone said, "Whaddaya mean by that?"

I grew agitated, restless, and insulting, permanently aggrieved. "How can you say that!" I cried
long before I could vote. I was beside myself with
my mother's sense of deprivation. It was as though
I'd been cheated at birth of the Ideal Friend, and
now all I could do was register the insufficiency of
the one at hand.

I was never going to know what Keats knew before he was twenty-five, that "any set of people is
as good as any other." Now *there* was a Shakespearean life. Keats occupied his own experience to such
a remarkable degree, he needed only the barest of
human exchanges to connect with an inner clarity
he himself had achieved. For that, almost anyone
would do. He lived inside the heaven of a mind
nourished by its own conversation. I would wander
for the rest of my life in the purgatory of self-exile,
always looking for the right person to talk to.

This dead end led quickly to high-minded mor-
alizing. I became the only fourteen-year-old girl on
the block who pronounced regularly on the meaning and nature of Love with a capital L. Real love,
true love, right love. You knew *instantly*, I declared
categorically, when you were in the presence of love.
If you didn't know, it wasn't love. If it *was*, whatever the obstacles, you were to give yourself to it
without question, because love was the supreme intensity, the significant exaltation. It was the cer-

tainty with which I rehearsed this litany, again and
again, that marked me.

At the same time that I was pontificating about
Love with a capital L, I was a girl who continually
daydreamed herself up on the stage of some great
auditorium, or on a platform in a public square, ad-
dressing a crowd of thousands, urging it to revolution. The conviction that one day I would have the
eloquence and the vision to move people to such
action was my secret thrill. Sometimes I'd feel puzzled about how I would manage life both as an
agent of revolution and as a devotee of Love. Inevitably, then, a picture formed itself of me on the
stage, my face glowing with purpose, and an ador-
ing man in the audience waiting for me to come
down into his arms. That seemed to cover all the
bases.

As I passed into my late teens, this image in my
head of myself leading the revolution began, mysteriously, to complicate itself. I knew, of course, that
a significant life included real work—work done
out in the world—but now I seemed to imagine that
an Ideal Partner was necessary in order to do the
work. With the right man at my side, I posited, I
could do it all. Without the right man . . . but no,
that was unthinkable. There would *be* no without
the right man. The emphasis began to shift away from
doing the work to finding the right man in order to

do the work. Slowly but surely, finding the right man seemed to become the work.

In college, the girls who were my friends were literary. Every one of us identified either with George Eliot's Dorothea Brooke, who mistakes a pedant for a man of intellect, or with Henry James's Isabel Archer, who sees the evil-hearted Osmond as a man of cultivation. Those who identified with Dorothea were impressed by her prideful devotion to "standards"; those who didn't thought her a provincial prig. Those who identified with Isabel admired her for the largeness of her emotional ambition; those who didn't thought her dangerously naïve. Either way, my friends and I saw ourselves as potential variations of one or the other. The seriousness of our concerns lay in our preoccupation with these two fictional women.

The problem, in both *Middlemarch* and *Portrait of a Lady*, was that of the protagonist—beautiful, intelligent, sensitive—mistaking the wrong man for the right man. As a problem, the situation seemed entirely reasonable to all of us. We saw it happening every day of the week. Among us were young women of grace, talent, and good looks attached, or becoming attached, to men dull in mind or spirit who were bound to drag them down. The prospect of such a fate haunted all of us. We each shuddered to think that we might become such women.

Not me, I determined. If I couldn't find the right man, I swore boldly, I'd do without.

For nearly ten years after college I knocked about in pursuit of the holy grail: Love with a capital L, Work with a capital W. I read, I wrote, I fell into bed. I was married for ten minutes, I smoked marijuana for five. Lively and animated, I roamed the streets of New York and Europe. Somehow, nothing quite suited. I couldn't figure out how to get down to work, and needless to say, I couldn't stumble on the right man. In time, a great lassitude overcame me. It was as though I'd fallen asleep on my feet and needed to be awakened.

On the very last day of my twenties I married a scientist, a man of brooding temperament who had taken eighteen years to complete his dissertation. His difficulty made him poetic in my eyes. He, of course, was remarkably sensitive to my own divided will. During our courtship we walked together by the hour while I discoursed ardently on why I could not get to Moscow. His eyes flashed with emotion as I spoke. "My dear girl!" he would exclaim. "My beautiful, marvelous girl. You are life itself!"

I became the interesting, conflicted personage and he the intelligent, responsive wife. The arrangement made us both happy. It felt like comradeship. At last, I thought, I had an Ideal Friend. Life seemed sweet then. Alone, I had been cramped up inside;

now I felt myself breathing freely. It gave me pleasure to open my eyes in the morning and see my
husband lying beside me. I experienced a comfort
of the soul that I had not known before.

One morning I awoke desolate. Why, I could not
tell. Nothing had changed. He was the same, I was
the same. Just a few weeks before I'd awakened feeling festive. Now I stood in the shower stricken,
spots of grief dancing in the air before my eyes, the
old loneliness seeping back in.

Who is he? I thought.

He's not the right one, I thought.

If only I had the right one, I thought.

A year later we were divorced.

I was still my mother's daughter. Now she was
the negative and I the print, but there we both were:
alone at last with not the right one.

I did not understand until years after I'd left
Gerald that I was born to find the wrong man, as
were Dorothea and Isabel. That's what we were in
business for. If this had not been the case, we'd all
have found some useful work to do and long forgotten the whole question of the right man. But we did
not forget it. We never forgot it. The elusive right
man became a staple in our lives, his absence a de-
fining experience.

It was then that I understood the fairy tale about
the princess and the pea. She wasn't after the prince,

she was after the pea. That moment when she feels the pea beneath the twenty mattresses, that is her moment of definition. It is the very meaning of her journey, why she has traveled so far, what she has come to confirm: the unholy dissatisfaction that will keep life permanently at bay.

So it was with my mother, who spent her years sighing for the absent right one. And so it was with me.

We were in thrall to neurotic longing, all of us—Dorothea and Isabel, my mother and I, the fairy-tale princess. Longing was what attracted us, what compelled our deepest attention. The essence, indeed, of a Chekhovian life. Think of all those Natashas sighing through three long acts for what is not, and can never be. While one (wrong) man after another listens sympathetically to the recital of a dilemma for which there is no solution.

Gerald and I were Natasha and the Doctor forever talking, talking, talking. Behind Natasha's enchanting conversation lies a passivity of monumental proportion—for which the Doctor is the perfect foil. Inevitably, Natasha and the Doctor must part. They have only been keeping each other company, spending their equally insufficient intent together.

•

A man and a woman sitting side by side on a bus strike up a conversation. She is black, middle-aged, well dressed; he is white, also middle-aged, slightly wild-eyed. Apropos of nothing he says to her, "I'm spiritual. I'm a very spiritual person. I accept all religions. All religions are okay by me. I hold only one thing against Christianity. Why they hate the Jews for killing Christ." The woman turns full face to him and says, "Y'know? I've always thought the same thing. After all, it was the Romans who killed him. Why don't they blame the Italians?"

•

If life begins to feel like the sum of its disabilities, I take a walk up to Times Square—home to the savviest underclass in the world—where I quickly regain perspective. On Broadway at Forty-Third Street on a windy evening in winter, a black man on a makeshift platform is speaking into a microphone. Ranged around the platform are perhaps a dozen black men and women. The man at the mike sounds like a television broadcaster. People hunched over against the wind are rushing past him, but he goes on speaking in the smooth, imperturbable tones of the evening news anchor. "It has come to my attention lately," he says, "that sales are up on suntan lotion and sunblock. Now who do you think are the customers for this item? I'll tell you who.

White people, that's who. Not you or I, brother. No, it's white people." His voice deepens. "Now what do you think of a people who keep telling us they're superior, and . . ." Without warning he pauses, his eyes squeeze shut, and he screams, *"They can't even make it in the fuckin' sun!"* Back to broadcast news. "You—" He points calmly at the heads of the fleeing crowd. "The white people. Don't even belong. On the planet."

•

When I ran into Manny Rader on Third Avenue, I hadn't seen him in twenty-five years. He was the older brother of the girl in the neighborhood who'd been my best friend when we were twelve. After I turned fourteen, he'd begun staring at me. As soon as I saw him on Third Avenue, I knew I had to have him.

I have a penchant for men I've grown up with. They're like chloroform on a cloth laid against my face: I inhale them, I burrow into them, I want to bury myself in them. When I was a kid I wanted to be them—these dark, skinny, street-smart boys with hot eyes and ignorant passions who came together every day at the top of the block to laugh, curse, and kibitz themselves into existence—I never got over not being one of them. It wasn't that I envied them their shared act of imagination—the one they seemed to have inherited, it came so naturally to them—it was that it frightened me when I realized I wasn't one of them, and never would be. I felt imperiled then: without world and without self.

"Who'd have thought you'd turn out a writer," Manny said to me on Third Avenue, a bemused expression on his face. And then he laughed. "You were such a pain in the ass as a kid, always hanging around where you weren't wanted." His laugh brought it all back to me, made me see those feelings again as though they were standing in the air before me. He had had this rich, deep laugh I used to hear when I'd pass the boys standing on the corner. Only his friends had made him laugh like that, never the girls.

We fell into bed and astonished ourselves with a strong, sweet happiness neither of us could have dreamed was coming. One afternoon when we were making love, I went down on him. As I came up I said, "The dream of every boy in the Bronx, that the girl down the street will suck him off." Manny lay back on the bed and laughed that unguarded, in-the-world laugh of his. It thrilled me more than anything our bodies were doing together. I stared at the wall beyond his head, thinking, I'm safe. Now he'll never leave me. But of course I didn't really think Manny was going to do the leaving; if anything, it would be me who skipped.

He had walked away from everything but the women all his life. He'd gone to college on a scholarship, then left in his third year to join the army; he'd entered business with a known embezzler, and within two years the business had gone under; he rose from technician to researcher in a biology lab, then got into a fight with his boss and quit; he worked on a large national magazine where he was quickly made reporter, then editor, and then fired because he disappeared for a week without explanation. On the block he was written off as a congenital fuckup. "He can't find himself," his mother moaned. "That's a nice way of putting it," his father sneered.

But his mother was right: Manny couldn't find himself. Whatever the circumstance that Manny found himself in, he couldn't find himself in it. He never repeated the same kind of work twice. Each job remained just that, a job. None of them ever became more than an apprenticeship. The events of his life refused to accumulate into experience, and he would not act as though they had. This inner refusal of his seemed to be his only gift. Certainly, it was the talent he pursued. By the time we began sleeping together, he was starting to tell himself that refusenik was his condition and his destiny. Even though he knew better, and being with me made him see even more clearly what he already knew.

When Manny and I hooked up, I was in a slump. That's how I put it. "I'm in a slump." Manny looked at me. "You're in a slump?" he said. "What does that mean? That's bullshit for you don't wanna work, right? That's what it means, doesn't it? It means you're a writer who doesn't write. Even I can see that. We're together now, what? Three months? I've been watching you. You don't even sit down at the desk. You fuck away the day, day after day. Every day, you fuck it away. You did a little work, got a little recognition, and that's it, right? You're finished. You got no more fight in you. Right? I mean, what *more* do they want from you? Am I right? Have I got that right?"

He took one look at my life, and sex gave him all the focus he needed. He saw the leakage in the pipeline, understood the drain of spirit in me. He sympathized with what he saw—the sympathy provided the connection between us as well as the heat—but he wasn't into euphemisms.

At forty-six, Manny was as skinny as he'd been at seventeen. I, as always, was fighting fifteen pounds of overweight. "Sweetheart," he murmured against my breasts, burying himself in me in that way that men do, "you're a Renoir." I've never understood what it is about female flesh that sends them off like that, but whenever Manny said this I would smile into the dark with relief. I needed him to lose himself in me. I was still buying time. And I still didn't understand for what I was buying it.

•

One year when I was teaching in Arizona, Leonard came out to visit me and we took a trip to the Grand Canyon, making a few stops here and there as we traveled across one of the most striking landscapes on earth. A day and a half into the trip, we came up over a rise, and there, as far as the eye could see, was the great western desert without a sign of human life on it. The sheer sweep of world without definition and without end took my breath away.

"How beautiful!" came out of my mouth before I even registered a thought.

Leonard was silent.

"No?" I inquired.

He smiled one of his small, tight smiles.

"What is it you feel?" he asked with genuine curiosity; he really wanted to know.

Now I felt obliged to think.

"Elated," I replied. "Inspirited."

Silence.

"Don't you?" I asked.

"Never," he replied, and shivered. "I feel awe looking at the elemental world," he said. "Fear, actually. Conversely, looking at a civilized landscape I feel moved by the human effort to push back the alienness. With me and nature it's either terror or gratitude. Inspirited, never."

•

On upper Broadway a beggar approaches a middle-aged woman. "I don't drink, I don't do drugs, I just need—," he starts. To his amazement, the woman yells directly into his face, "I just had my pocket picked!" The beggar turns his face northward and calls to a colleague up the block, "Hey, Bobby, leave her alone, she just got robbed."

•

It was through the discovery and exploration of the unconscious that Freud made his major discoveries, chief among them that from birth to death we are, every last one of us, divided against ourselves. We both want to grow up and don't want to grow up; we hunger for sexual pleasure, we dread sexual pleasure; we hate our own aggressions—anger, cruelty, the need to humiliate—yet they derive from the grievances we are least willing to part with. Our very suffering is a source of both pain and reassurance. What Freud found most difficult to cure in his patients was the resistance to being cured.

•

I had a friend once with whom I was certain I would grow old. My friendship with Emma was not one I would have described as Montaigne does his with Étienne de La Boétie—as one in which the soul grows refined—but now that I am thinking about it, I see that, in important ways, it was analogous. Ours was an attachment that, if it did not refine the soul, certainly nourished the spirit so well that, for a very long time indeed, we each seemed to experience our inquiring selves fully in the presence of the other. At school we'd both been prime examples of those very intelligent girls whose insecurities equip them with voices that easily generate scorn and judgment. It would be years before those formidable defenses altered sufficiently that each of us could see herself in the other. I remember once when we were in our twenties hearing Emma correct someone's grammar—"The word is *who*, not *whom*"—and the contempt in her voice made me wince. Thank God *I* don't sound like that, I thought. But I did. We were in our thirties when I first heard myself as I heard Emma whenever one or the other of us said some awful thing. And then the corrective of self-recognition—a thrilling occurrence at that point in our lives—worked a kind of magic between us. In no time at all it became necessary for us to meet or speak at least three times a week. The open road of friendship everlasting seemed spread out before us.

To the uninitiated eye, this vitality of connection between Emma and me might have appeared puzzling. She was a bourgeois through and through, I a radical feminist who owned nothing. She had married, become a mother, and pursued graduate work; I was twice divorced, had remained childless, and lived the marginal existence of a working freelance. Beneath these separating realities, however, lay a single compelling influence that drew us irresistibly toward each other.

Together, we seemed always to be puzzling out those parts of the general condition to which our own circumstances applied. Emma had embraced the family, I had rejected the family; she endorsed the middle class, I loathed the middle class; she dreaded loneliness, I endured it. Yet the longer we went on meeting and talking, the more clearly we saw that to know how we had come to be as we were was for both of us the central enterprise. When we spoke together of the exhaustion of love and the anguish of work, the smell of children and the taste of solitude, we were really speaking of the search for the self and the confusion that came with the mere construction of the phrase: What *was* the self? Where was it? How did one pursue it, abandon or betray it? These questions were the ones that concentrated our deepest concerns. Consciousness as a first value, we each discovered, was what we together were exploring.

The absorption grew in us day by month by year, fed by the excitement of abstract thought joined to the concreteness of daily life. In conversation with each other, we both felt the strength of context imposed on the quotidian. The more we explored the immediate in service to the theoretical—a chance encounter on the bus, a book just begun or just finished, a dinner party gone bad—the larger the world seemed to grow. The everyday became raw material for a developing perspective that was acquiring narrative drive: sitting in a living room, eating in a restaurant, walking in the street—it was as though we had grasped things whole without ever having had to leave home.

We went on like this for nearly ten years. And then one day the bond between us began to unravel. I had a bad exchange with Emma's husband, and she saw it as divisive. She read a book by a liberationist writer I prized, and I was stung by her scorn. We each made a new friend whose virtues the other failed to respond to. That winter I could barely pay the rent, and Emma's preoccupation with redecorating her place got under my skin. Suddenly, the adventure we had made of our differing circumstances seemed to be going sour: my cozy apartment felt sterile, her amiable husband a fool. Who *are* we? I remember thinking. What are we doing? And why are we doing it together?

Slowly but inexorably, the enterprise of mind and spirit to which our friendship had been devoted began to lose strength before the growing encroachment of the sympathies out of which our lives were actually fashioned. Like an uncontrollable growth that overtakes a clearing in the forest, the differences moved in on us. In no time at all, the friendship that had for so long generated excitement and exerted power was now experienced as a need that had run its course. Overnight, it seemed, it took one long stride and moved from the urgent center to the exhausted margin. Just like sexual infatuation, I remember thinking idly one morning as I lay in bed staring at the ceiling. And then, somewhat dazedly, I realized, That's right. That's exactly what this is like. Sexual infatuation.

In the end, my friendship with Emma did prove to bear a striking resemblance to romantic love. The passion that had flared between us now seemed an equivalent of the kind of erotic feeling that dies of its own intensity at the moment one begins to realize that much in oneself is not being addressed by this attraction of the senses. The irony here was that sexual love usually fails because of an insufficiency of shared sensibility, whereas sensibility was what Emma and I had had in abundance.

When my friendship with Emma was disintegrating, I recalled Winston Churchill's having once said there are no permanent friends, only permanent interests, and although I understood that Churchill meant worldly ambition trumps personal loyalties, I remember thinking even then, He's wrong, there are no permanent interests, either. It was the infidelity of our own mutating "interests" that had brought me and Emma low.

Our inner lives, William James announced, are fluid, restless, mercurial, always in transition. The transitions, he speculated, are the reality, and concluded that our experience "lives in the transitions." This is a piece of information difficult to absorb, much less accept, yet it is transparently persuasive. How else account for the mysterious shift in emotional sympathies that, at any hour of the ordinary day, brings a marriage, a friendship, a professional connection that has repeatedly threatened dissolution, to a "sudden" actual end?

The withdrawal of feeling in romantic love is a drama most of us are familiar with and therefore feel equipped to explain. In thrall to the intensity generated by passion, we invest love with transformative powers; imagine ourselves about to be made new, even whole, under its influence. When the expected transformation fails to materialize, the hopes interwoven with the infatuation do a desperate dissolve. The adventure of having felt known in the presence of the lover now bleeds out into the anxiety of feeling exposed.

In both friendship and love, the expectation that one's expressive (if not best) self will flower in the presence of the beloved other is key. Upon that flowering all is posited. But what if the restless, the fluid, the mercurial, within each of us is steadily undermining the very thing we think we most want? What, in fact, if the assumption of a self in *need* of expressiveness is an illusion? What if the urge toward stable intimacy is perpetually threatened by an equally great, if not greater, urge toward destabilization? What then?

•

On Fourteenth Street, at noon on a summer's day—in the midst of honking traffic, bargain store shoppers, crosstown bus riders—I run into Victor, an unhappy dentist who has lived in my neighborhood for years. Tall and slim, with a Caesar haircut and sad brown eyes, he is a nervous man who smiles compulsively. Whenever he sees me he coos, "Dahling, sweetness, beautiful girl, how a-a-are you?" Then, like a mother in a permanent state of interested alarm, he peers intently into my face and very gently asks, "You still writing, dahling?" Some years ago Victor, in search of inner peace, began traveling regularly to Japan to consult the Zen healer who has given him the wherewithal to get out of bed in the morning in New York. He must be sixty by now.

Standing here on Fourteenth Street, a Con Ed drill blasting in our ears, Victor croons at me, "Dahling, sweetness, beautiful girl, how *are* you, still living in the same building?"

"Yes," I reply.

"Still doing journalistic work?"

"No, Victor, I teach now."

He pushes his chin out at me as though to say, "Tell me."

I tell him. He listens intently as the words fall rapidly from my mouth, nodding steadily as I speak of the deprivation of spirit I suffer living for months at a time in one university town or another.

"It's exile!" I cry at last. "Exile pure and simple."

Victor nods and nods. His brown eyes are dissolving in watery pain. He knows *exactly* what I mean, oh, no one in the world will ever know better than he what I mean. His face goes dreamy. My own starts feeling compromised. Car brakes screech, sirens pierce the air, the Con Ed drill stops and starts, stops and starts. No matter. Victor and I are now quarantined on this island of noise, spellbound by matters of the soul.

"But you know, dahling?" he says ever so softly. "I have discovered there's a lot of love out there."

"Oh yes," I reply quickly, suddenly aware of the harm my relentless negatives may be doing.

"A lot of love," he repeats reverentially.

"Absolutely," I agree. "Absolutely."

The Con Ed drill starts up again.

"I mean, people *care*." By now Victor's face is radiant. "They really do."

And it is me who is nodding and nodding.

Victor puts his hand on my arm, leans toward me, looks searchingly into my eyes, and delivers himself of his wisdom.

"Dahling," he whispers in my ear, "we've got to let it go."

Yes, yes, oh yes, I know just what you mean.

"Let it all *go*."

•

After 9/11, an atmosphere difficult to describe enveloped the city and refused to abate. For weeks on end the town felt vacant, confused, uprooted. People walked around looking spaced-out, as though permanently puzzled by something they couldn't put a name to. The smell was eerie: like nothing anybody could describe exactly, but when your nostrils inhaled the air, you felt anxious. And all the while a kind of otherworldly quiet prevailed. In restaurants, theaters, museums; shops, traffic, the crowd itself—all seemed muted, inert, even immobilized. A man who loved New York movies found himself turning the television set off when one came on. A woman who enjoyed seeing photographs of the city in a storefront she passed daily now flinched as she approached the shop. The pictures, she said, felt like "before," and nothing "before" gave comfort.

One soft, clear evening about six weeks after the fateful day, I was crossing Broadway, somewhere in the Seventies. Halfway across, the light changed. I stopped on the island that divides the boulevard and did what everyone does: looked down the street for a break in the traffic so that I could safely run the light. But there was no traffic: not a car in sight. I stood there, hypnotized by the grand and awful emptiness. I couldn't recall the time—except for a blizzard, perhaps—when Broadway had ever, even for a moment, been free of oncoming traffic. It looked like a scene from another time. Just like a Berenice Ab—, I started thinking, and instantly the thought cut itself short. In fact, I wrenched myself from it. I saw that it was frightening me to even consider "a scene from another time." As though some fatal break had occurred between me and the right to yearn over that long-ago New York alive in a Berenice Abbot photograph. That

night I understood what it was that had been draining out of the city throughout this sad, stunned
season.

When human experience slides off the scale,
and the end of civilization threatens, only hard
truths will do; and I was finding them sealed into
the minimalist prose of French and Italian novelists
of the fifties and sixties. Here, an eerie inwardness
trapped in the prose resonated inside a suffusing
silence that promised moral disorder of a serious
nature. Ah yes, the reader feels. However it once
was, that's the way it is now.

Standing there on the island in the middle of
Broadway, I realized what it was that we were losing: it was nostalgia. And then I realized that it
was *this* that was at the heart of postwar fiction. It
wasn't sentiment that was missing from these novels, it was nostalgia. That cold, pure silence at the
heart of modern European prose is the absence of
nostalgia: an absence made available only to those
who feel themselves standing at the end of history,
staring, without longing or regret, into the is-ness
of what is. Now, here in New York after 9/11, if
only for the moment, we too stood, lined up with
the rest of a world permanently postwar, staring
into that cold, silent purity.

•

Late for an appointment in midtown, I run down the subway stairs just as the train is pulling into the Fourteenth Street station. The doors open and a young man standing in front of me (T-shirt, jeans, crew cut) with an elaborately folded-up baby carriage on his back, leading a very small child by the hand, heads for the seats directly ahead of us. I plop down on the one opposite him, take out my book and reading glasses, and, settling myself, am vaguely aware of the man removing the carriage from his back and turning toward the seated child. Then I look up. The little boy is about seven or eight, and he is the most grotesquely deformed child I have ever seen. He has the face of a gargoyle—mouth twisted to the side, one eye higher than the other—inside a huge, misshapen head that reminds me of the Elephant Man. Bound around the child's neck is a narrow piece of white cloth, in the center of which sits a short, fat tube that seems to be inserted into his throat. In another instant I realize that he is also deaf. This last because the man immediately begins signing. At first, the boy merely watches the man's moving fingers, but soon he begins responding with motions of his own. Then, as the man's fingers move more and more rapidly, the boy's quicken, and within minutes both sets of fingers are matched in speed and complexity.

Embarrassed at first to be watching these two so steadily, I keep turning away, but they are so clearly

oblivious to everyone around them that I can't re-
sist looking up repeatedly from my book. And then
something remarkable happens: the man's face is
suffused with such delight and affection as the
boy's responses grow ever more animated—the
twisted little mouth grinning, the unaligned eyes
brightening—that the child himself begins to look
transformed. As the stations go by, and the conversation between the man and the boy grows ever
more absorbing to them, fingers flying, both nodding
and laughing, I find myself thinking, These two are
humanizing each other at a very high level.

By the time we get to Fifty-Ninth Street, the boy
looks beautiful to me, and the man beatific.

•

My mother had heart surgery. She emerged from
the operation in a state of calm I'd never known her
to possess. Criticism and complaint disappeared
from her voice, grievance from her face. Everything
was a matter of interest to her: negotiating the bus,
the sunlight on her cheeks, the bread in her mouth.
In a diner before we are due to take a bus ride across
town, she sips her coffee appreciatively (usually she
complains it's not hot enough) and eats a pastry
with relish. She sits back, beaming at me. Then
she leans across the table and declares vehemently,
"This is the best cheese Danish I have ever eaten."

We leave the diner and walk to the bus stop. "Let's stand here," she says, pointing to a spot a few feet beyond the sign. "It used to throw me into a rage," she explains, "that the driver would always pass the sign and stop here. I never understood why. But now I realize that it is actually easier for him to lower the step here for people like me than it is at the sign." She laughs and says, "I've noticed lately that when I don't get angry I have more thoughts than when I do. It makes life interesting."

I nearly weep. All I had ever wanted was that my mother be glad to be alive in my presence. I am still certain that if she had been, I'd have grown up whole inside.

"Imagine," I say to Leonard. "She's so old and she can still do this to me."

"It's not how old she is that's remarkable," he says. "It's how old *you* are."

•

A month ago, I passed a middle-aged couple on the promenade at Battery Park City. She was black, he white; both had gray hair and wavy jawlines. They were holding hands and talking earnestly, their eyes searching each other's faces for the answers to questions that only lovers put to each other. I realized, as I looked at them, that the city now contains a considerable number of middle-aged interracial couples.

I'd been spotting them all over town for more than a year now, black men and white women, white men and black women, almost all of them in their forties or fifties, clearly in the first stages of intimacy. It moved me to be reminded once again of how long it is taking blacks and whites to become real to one another.

·

At ten in the morning, as I am standing on line in my branch library, waiting to check out a book, a frail-looking woman about my own age suddenly grasps the edge of the checkout desk and remains standing there. I lean forward from my place in the line and call out to her, "Is everything all right?" She glances wanly in my direction, then screams at me, "Why the *hell* are you asking me if everything is all right?"

At noon, waiting on the corner for the light to change, I look down and see a pair of shoes I think beautiful but complicated. "Are those shoes comfortable?" I inquire of the young woman wearing them. She backs off, looks at me with suspicion in her eyes, and in an alarmed voice says, "Why are you asking me that?"

At three in the afternoon, I pass a man who is yelling into the air, "Help me! Help me! I've got four uncurable diseases! Help me!" I tap him on the shoulder and cheerfully confide, "The word is *incurable*." Without missing a beat, he replies, "Who the fuck asked you."

The randomness of life being what it is, a few days later I have another "who the fuck asked you" day.

I'm sitting in an aisle seat on a crosstown bus. A man—black, somewhere in his forties, dressed in jeans and an oversize yellow T-shirt—is standing beside me, speaking very loudly into a cell phone.

I catch his eye and make a motion with my hand that means, "Lower your voice." He looks amazed.

"Lower my voice?" he says incredulously. "No, madam, I will *not* lower my voice. I paid my fare, I'll do what I damned please."

"Your fare entitles you to ride the bus," I reply. "It does not entitle you to hold the passengers hostage."

"Why, you bitch," the man cries.

I leave my seat and go up to the driver. "Did you hear what that man just said to me?"

"Yes, lady," the driver says wearily. "I heard him."

"Are you going to do anything about it?" I demand.

"What do you want me to do? Call the police?"

"You bitch, you white bitch," the man on the cell phone howls.

"Yes," I say, "call the police."

The bus grinds to a halt.

"Everybody off the bus," the driver calls out.

A woman in the back wails, "I'm late for my therapist!"

When the cops show up, they laugh at me.

I go home, write up the incident, and e-mail it to the *Times*.

Two days later, my phone rings and a man from the paper says, "You want us to publish *this*?"

•

She was born Mary Britton Miller in New London, Connecticut, in 1883, into a wealthy Protestant family and grew up to become one of the Odd Women. Who can say why. Her childhood was marked by humdrum melodrama—by the age of three she'd been orphaned, at fourteen her twin sister drowned, by eighteen (it's been speculated) she might have borne an illegitimate baby. What, however, can actually account for a sensibility destined to be shaped by one set of experiences rather than another; or, for that matter, explain why one set of events rather than another *becomes* experience. What is certain, however, is that inevitably one ends up deeply surprised— "This is *not* what I had in mind!"—at how it has all turned out; and just as inevitably, the surprise becomes one's raw material.

Whatever the truth of her inner circumstance, in 1911, at the age of twenty-eight, Mary Miller settled in New York City, where she worked and lived, quite alone, for the rest of her long life. When she died in 1975, it was in the Greenwich Village apartment she had occupied for more than forty years. She was never married, and she seems not to have had a lover anyone ever knew. What she did have was friends, some of whom described her as witty and mean, entertainingly haughty, and impressively self-educated.

For years, Mary B. Miller wrote conventional poems and stories that got published but went unnoticed. Then, between 1946 and 1952, between the ages of sixty-three and sixty-nine, under the name of Isabel Bolton, she produced three short modernist novels that, at the time of publication, earned her a significant amount of literary attention. Edmund Wilson praised her work in *The New Yorker*, as did Diana Trilling in *The Nation*. Both critics thought they had discovered a major new talent.

These novels are all voice, hardly any plot at all. The reader is inside the mind of a woman— essentially it's the same woman in all the books— going through a day (or a few days) in New York, musing, thinking, reminiscing, trying to puzzle out her life in prose that mimics interiority: free, flashing, reverie-bound. The action is always at a remove; it is the reverie that counts. In the first novel the year is 1939, the woman is in her forties, and she's named Millicent. In the second it's 1945, she's

in her fifties and named Hilly. In the third it's 1950,
she's in her eighties, and she's Margaret. A life dot-
ted with smart, knowing New Yorkers is sketched
in, characters are scattered about, and always there
is a young man to whom the protagonist is oddly
attached; but really she is alone, and has been alone
forever. In each story, however, the woman is able to
cut a deal with life because she has the city to love.
And how she loves it:

> What a strange, what a fantastic city . . .
> there was something here that one experi-
> enced nowhere else on earth. Something one
> loved intensely. What was it? Crossing the
> streets—standing on the street corners with
> the crowds: what was it that induced this
> special climate of the nerves . . . a peculiar
> sense of intimacy, friendliness, being here
> with all these people and in this strange
> place . . . They touched your heart with ten-
> derness and you felt yourself a part of the
> real flight and flutter—searching their faces,
> speculating about their dooms and destinies.

This relation between the self and the city is
Bolton's true subject, the modernist part of her
enterprise:

You ran about in motor cars, you boarded
ocean liners, crossed the continent in Chiefs
and Super Chiefs . . . the present moment so
filled with terror and tenderness, and experiencing every day such a queer intensity. Wondering so often who you were and what you
were and who it might be necessary for you
to be the next moment . . . and the heart so
hungry for heaven knew just what, so unas-
suaged, so void . . . [But then] almost anything might happen to you in New York . . .
the fabulous city like a great Christmas
tree, so brilliantly lighted, with so many glittering gifts perpetually being handed out . . .
You wouldn't call it the natural climate of
your soul . . . Longing as you were for some
display of natural warmth and friendli-
ness [that seemed] to have dissolved in gos-
sip, analysis—sophistication . . . There was
hunger, there was immense curiosity, there
was solitude . . . Yet there were these sudden, these unaccountable moments—being
overtaken by love—everywhere—on top of
buses, in crowded concert halls—sometimes
on winter evenings with the skyscrapers floating, flickering above you . . . merging with
the crowds, examining the faces. This sense

of brotherhood. You buried your loneliness
in it.

This was the loneliness that told Bolton she was
"the most solitary . . . individual that ever at any
moment in the march of mad events had trod upon
the earth."

Then the paradox of her situation hits her:
"Christ, how we loved our own aloneness . . . We
were incapable of giving because there was so much
within our reach to grab and snatch and gather for
our own, our solitary souls."

Bolton was nearly seventy when she wrote these
words. She had lived long enough to see that modern life, with its unspeakable freedoms mirrored in
the gorgeous disconnect of the crowded city, has re-
vealed us to ourselves as has the culture of no other
age. She sees what Freud saw—that our loneliness
is anguishing and yet, inexplicably, we are loath to
give it up. At no period in psychological time are we
free of the contradiction: it is the conflict of conflicts. This was Bolton's wisdom, her only wisdom.
When she wrote it in the late 1940s it sounded profound to her most literate readers.

•

The two greatest writers of the urban crowd in the
nineteenth century were Charles Dickens and Victor

Hugo. Each, in his own way, had grasped whole the meaning of these metropolitan masses rapidly developing in London and in Paris. Dickens especially understood its significance. To see a swiftly moving man or woman out of the side of your eye—to feel his or her presence at an angle of vision that allowed one to register only half a face, part of an expression, a piece of a gesture; and then to have to decide quickly how to react to this flood of human partialness—this was creating a radical change in social history.

Victor Hugo, along with many other nineteenth-century writers, saw the same thing and understood, as Walter Benjamin put it, that there was no subject more entitled to his attention than the crowd. It was Hugo's shrewdness, Benjamin wrote, that made him see the crowd "was getting ready to take shape as a public . . . who had acquired facility in reading" and was becoming the kind of purchaser of books that "wished to find itself portrayed in the contemporary novel, as the patrons did in the paintings of the Middle Ages."

These remarks of Benjamin's on Victor Hugo occur in a famous essay he wrote on Baudelaire, the writer who meant the most to him. It was in Baudelaire that the idea of the flaneur developed: that is, the person who strolls aimlessly through the streets of the big cities in studied contrast with the hurried, purposeful activity of the crowd. It was the flaneur, Baudelaire thought, who would morph into the writer of the future. "Who among us," he wrote, "has not dreamt, in his ambitious days, of the miracle of a poetic prose . . . [that would] adapt itself to the lyrical stirrings of the soul, the wave motions of dreaming, the shocks of consciousness. This ideal . . . will grip especially those who are at home in the giant cities and the web of their numberless interconnecting relationships." This crowd, Benjamin wrote, of whose existence Baudelaire is always aware, "has not served as the model for any of his works, but it is imprinted on his creativity as a hidden figure."

I'm walking up Fifth Avenue at noon straight into the cold hard sunlight of a morning in November. Mobs of people are coming at me. Once the dominating color of this crowd was white, now it is black and brown. Once it wore blue and white collars, now it is in mufti. Once it was law-abiding, now it is not. The idiom has changed, but the character remains stable. Every now and then I see a face and a figure mixed in among the regulation jeans and parkas—something narrow faced and creamy skinned in glossy furs (Paris, 1938); something swarthy and dangerous in island Spanish (Cuba, 1952); something sloe-eyed and timeless (Egypt, 4000 B.C.)—and I am reminded of the enduring nature of the crowd. New York belongs to me as much as it does to them: but no more so. We are all here on Fifth Avenue for the same reason and by virtue of the same right. We have all been walking the streets of world capitals forever: actors, clerks, criminals; dissidents, runaways, illegals; Nebraska gays, Polish intellectuals, women on the edge of time. Half of these people will be lost to glitter and crime—disappearing into Wall Street, hiding out in Queens—but half of them will become me: a walker in the city; here to feed the never-ending stream of the never-ending crowd that is certainly imprinting on *someone's* creativity.

•

Leonard and I are passing a bookstore. In its window we see a display of a book on cosmetic surgery written by a woman I know.

"She's only forty-two," I say. "Why is she writing about cosmetic surgery?"

"Maybe she's seventy," Leonard says. "What do you know?"

•

A writer of my acquaintance (I'll call her Alice) was felled at eighty-five by infirmity. Arthritis had attacked her from head to toe and left her so crippled that she had herself admitted to an assisted living facility in upper Manhattan. Composed of about a hundred studio apartments, a complete set of common rooms, a bright and airy dining room, the facility was both comfortable and attractive. Equipped (as it was) with excellent care, the place at first seemed a dream come true: a worthy woman laid low was being admirably attended to in her hour of need. But this facility was run by a development company heavily supported by federal moneys: which meant that differences in class, wealth, and education were reduced to accommodate a culture of the lowest common denominator. Therein lay the tale of a dream gone bad.

Alice, who was some twenty years older than me, had been a writer of reputation thirty years before the time I knew her. When I was in college my friends and I read her novels with interest and admiration. She was also glamorous. A slender woman with marvelous hair and great taste in clothes, she had a handsome husband, a house in the Hamptons, and an apartment in the Dakota. I didn't get to know her until she was nearly eighty, by which time her fortunes had reversed themselves. Her books were no longer being published, her husband had left her, and she was living in a residence for women.

Ours was one of those peculiar friendships based not on shared sensibility, but on the complications of emotional need. Shortly after Alice and

I met I found that I actually didn't like her. Her mind was alert, her mental energy intact, and her desire for conversation as alive as it had ever been. It was her manner (haughty), her politics (conservative), her literary taste (middlebrow) that put me off. We were both hot-tempered, so our conversations often dissolved in a wrangle of irritated disagreement, and more often than not I went home feeling both guilty and ashamed. Nonetheless, we continued to call ourselves friends. She badly needed an interlocutor who knew who she was, I badly needed to go on paying tribute to a writer who'd once meant a great deal to me.

I went to visit Alice two weeks after she entered the assisted living facility. The lobby, painted a soft yellow and furnished with brightly colored sofas and love seats, did have a few slack-faced women and men sitting listlessly about—Not a good omen, passed through my head—but the studio apartment that Alice had been given was lovely. Flooded with light and furnished in excellent taste, it seemed perfect: everything close to hand and good to look at. Alice herself seemed as well as a woman in constant pain could be. I asked how she was, and in ten minutes she told me. Then she said, "Enough of that," and she meant it. In no time we were talking as we always had about books, people we knew, that day's headlines. At five thirty she said, "Time for dinner."

I helped her out of her chair and handed her her cane; as we left the apartment, I remember thinking that she—tall, dignified, well dressed—was looking particularly alert.

The door to the dining room opened, and I nearly went into shock. The room was a forest of wheelchairs, walkers, and canes, most of the people attached to them looking as slack-jawed as those I'd seen in the lobby. As cheerfully painted and furnished as the room itself was, a look of dereliction— even destitution—suffused the place. It was the destitution of people who had been flung together simply because they were old and physically incapacitated.

Without a word, Alice guided me to two empty chairs at a table for six. The other four chairs were occupied by two men and two women, all of whom were silent. When we sat down their faces brightened and one of the men said, "Ah, here's Alice. *She'll* tell us what the right and the wrong of the matter is."

The matter turned out to concern an appetizer that had been wrongly delivered to Monica, the ninety-year-old redhead dressed in purple print polyester, when it should have gone to Minna, whose mouth trembled and whose blue eyes were awash in anxiety. It seemed that when Minna had asked the waitress to bring another appetizer for her, she was told that Monica was eating the last one. Here Minna had gone into free fall and had been insisting repeatedly that the dish should have come to *her*, not to Monica, it wasn't fair, it just wasn't fair. Alice instantly soothed Minna by telling her that it definitely was not fair, but that life itself was not fair, so experiencing this lack of fairness once *again* was proof that she was still alive; that alone should make her grateful. Minna's face broke into an enchanting smile, and the crisis was over.

A few weeks later I was again in the dining room with Alice, and again I witnessed people turning to her to adjudicate a dispute similar to the one that had involved Minna and Monica. This time it was an argument over a movie that had sent the whole table into a spin. "It's so interesting, don't you think?" Alice said to me as we left the room. I nodded silently. "The extraordinary things one learns about human behavior in a place like this," she said.

Possessed now of a stoic character I had never before seen in action, Alice was becoming a beloved figure in the facility. She had decided to take an interest in her surroundings, and her novelist's delight in the oddities of humanity at large had come to her aid. As a result, her old above-the-fray manner now came across as Solomonic. For the volatile residents of this place, the gravity of Alice's manner endowed her with a wisdom they instinctively felt they could trust. What's more, she was a genuine lady, wasn't she, the kind who honored the essential humanity of every person who crossed her field of vision. When Alice entered the dining room, people she didn't know smiled and nodded at her as she passed.

But the essential humanity of Alice herself was not being served. Each time I came to visit, she looked exponentially more weary than the time before. She was of course now well over eighty-five and living on painkillers; the weariness, however, was, in the main, of the spirit not the body. After some months in the facility, I'd find her slumped in her chair, looking so exhausted that it would scare me. Nevertheless, I'd sit down on a chair facing hers and, without even asking how she was, start talking. Within minutes of hearing my voice, her face, her body, the movement of her hands, began coming back to life. Soon we were conversing about books and headlines and people we knew as animatedly as we ever did, minus the wrangling. I don't think I'll ever forget the sight of that miraculous conversion. To see the engagement of a talented mind bring a half-dead person back to living liveliness was to witness a transformation that never felt less than magical.

"Is there no one here with whom you can have a conversation?" I once asked.

"No, dear," Alice replied. "Chatter, yes. I get

plenty of that. But conversation? No. Certainly not conversation like the one we are having."

The small talk that daily filled her ears, she told me, was deadening. Worse than silence, she said. Much worse.

A mutual friend surprised me by remarking on how sad it was that Alice's life should be winding down this way, by which our friend meant the failure of her marriage and the end of her literary career. But Alice's losses late in life were not at all to the point as far as I was concerned. After all, she had had a very good time for many years—money, glamour, reputation, steady sex—so what if it didn't see her through to the end? That was simply the roller-coaster ride of life common to us all, not actually a cause for sorrow. No, what mattered here was that Alice had spent a lifetime struggling to become a conscious human being whose primary delight was the use of her own mind; and now she was locked up in an atmosphere constructed to ignore—nay, discard—that long, valiant effort, when the only thing owed a human being—yes, from first to last—was to have it honored.

I felt the paltriness then of all my former complaints about this friendship. How mean and trivial they seemed; ignoble, really. All that mattered now was my friend's consignment—when not reading—to an exile of the mind that amounted to solitary confinement. It was as though Alice were being found guilty of having stayed alive too long. How strongly I felt the punishment in excess of the crime!

Alice lived on in the facility for seven more years. At her funeral I discovered that the most unlikely people had also visited her regularly. I knew most of them en passant, and none, I thought, had been any closer to her than I had been—a Village feminist, a performance artist from SoHo, a cousin up in the Bronx, a program director at the public library—yet it seemed we had all shared in a fellowship devoted to the rescue of Alice-in-solitary.

An image crossed my mind then of a circle laid down on the surface of Manhattan, with lines radiating out from the middle to the periphery. At any given moment someone in the fellowship was walking one of those lines toward the center where Alice stood waiting. When the fellow reached her, the line lit up.

•

In summer, in the tenement neighborhoods on the West Side, men play dominoes at card tables set up on the pavement, women sit talking on the stoop, kids play ball, teenagers make love, and everywhere people drink, smoke, do drugs. I once saw a pig being roasted at midnight in the middle of the street because someone had won the lottery. Throughout the day and most of the night, men and women screech, sob, laugh, quarrel at a high pitch. Emotions are unfiltered here and race about without nuance or restraint.

One evening in July, walking down Ninth Avenue in the Forties, the street thronged with people, I saw a man and a woman standing perfectly still in the crowd. He was looking intently at her face and had a hand pressed to her arm. She, in turn, had her face twisted away from his, her eyes pressed shut, her mouth forming a wordless *no*. As I came abreast of them, I happened to look up and I saw a woman on a fire escape staring down with hot eyes at the man and the woman in the street, the pain in her face unmistakable. For a moment I was jealous of life in Hell's Kitchen.

•

The street keeps moving, and you've got to love the movement. You've got to find the composition of the rhythm, lift the story from the motion, understand and not regret that the power of narrative drive is fragile, though infinite. Civilization is breaking up? The city is deranged? The century surreal? Move faster. Find the story line more quickly.

On the Sixth Avenue bus, I get up to give an old woman my seat. She's small and blond, wearing gold jewelry and a ratty mink coat, her hands a pair of blotchy claws with long red fingernails attached to them. "You did a good thing, dear," she says to me, and smiles coyly. "I'm ninety years old. I was ninety yesterday." I smile at her. "You look fantastic," I say, "not a day over seventy-five." Her eyes flash. "Don't get smart," she says.

At a coffee counter, two women sit talking at right angles to me. One is telling the other that a woman they both know is sleeping with a much younger man. "We all tell her, he wants your money." The woman speaking nods her head like a rag doll and lets her face go daffy in imitation of the woman she's speaking of. " 'Right,' she tells us, 'and he can *have* it, *all* of it.' Meanwhile, she looks great."

At Forty-Second Street, a man in front of me—skinny, young, black—suddenly lies down spread-eagle in the middle of the street just as the cars are beginning to move. I turn wildly to the man walking beside me, who, as it happens, is also skinny, young, black, and cry out at him, "Why is he *doing* this?" Without breaking his stride, he shrugs at me. "I don't know, lady. Maybe he's depressed."

Each day when I leave the house, I tell myself I'm going to walk up the East Side of town because the East Side is calmer, cleaner, more spacious. Yet I seem always to find myself on the crowded, filthy, volatile West Side. On the West Side life feels positively thematic. All that intelligence trapped inside all those smarts. It reminds me of why I walk. Why everyone walks.

•

When I was eight years old my mother cut a piece out of a dress I had been longing to wear to a friend's birthday party. She grabbed a pair of sewing scissors and sliced the part of the dress that would have covered my heart if, as she said, I had had one. "You're killing me," she always howled, eyes squeezed shut, fists clenched, when I disobeyed her or demanded an explanation she couldn't supply or nagged for something she wasn't going to give me. "Any minute now I'll be dead on the floor," she screamed that day, "you're so heartless." Needless to say, I did not go to the party. Instead I cried for a week and grieved over the incident for fifty years.

"How could you do that to a child?" I asked in later years, once when I was eighteen, again when I was thirty, yet again when I was forty-eight.

The odd thing was that each time I raised the incident my mother would say, "That never happened." I'd look at her then, more scornfully each time, and let her know in no uncertain terms that I was going to go on reminding her of this crime against childhood until one of us was dead.

As the years passed and I regularly brought up the memory of the dress cutting, she just as regularly denied its veracity. So we went on, with me not believing her, and not believing her, and not believing her. Then one day, quite suddenly, I did. On a cold spring afternoon in my late fifties, I stepped off the Twenty-Third Street crosstown bus at Ninth Avenue, and as my foot hit the ground I realized that whatever it was that *had* happened that day more than half a century ago, it wasn't at all what I remembered happening.

Migod, I thought, palm clapped to forehead, it's as though I were born to manufacture my own grievance. But why? And hold on to it for dear life. Again, why? When my hand came away from my forehead, I tipped an invisible hat to Leonard. Me too, I said silently to him. "So old and still with so little information."

•

For the longest time, the strong, sweet happiness Manny Rader and I experienced that first night we lay down together continued to exert itself. Romantic feeling welled up in each of us with astonishing regularity: in elevators, at bus stops, in restaurant doorways, in the darkness of the movie house, in the glare of an all-night diner. Suddenly, from one or the other of us would burst, "I love you oh God I love you I can't believe how much I love you." It was hard to account for the irrational swell of joy we called love, much less for how entirely it overtook me. I remember thinking, Is this what besotted means?

Manny had survived his long, puzzling melancholy by imagining himself perpetually poised for a future that had thus far eluded him. This meant making just enough money to survive and remaining marginal in all his habits. Still waiting for his life to begin, he did everything on the cheap. He drank coffee at a stand-up counter, walked everywhere he had to go, wore his clothes to shreds. The Staten Island ferry was our pleasure boat, student concerts at Juilliard our Carnegie Hall. Twofers at the theater, dinner at the diner, and excursion walks all over the city completed our social agenda.

My own insecurity about money was ever-present, but I lived in a fine apartment, ate in restaurants many times a week, and spent a small but considerable sum on music, theater, and the movies. Yet Manny's predilections invaded me easily. I fell in with them as though between this moment and the time we'd both been living in the Bronx nothing had intervened; as if I'd only learned to ape the manners of the middle class and were now reverting to type.

It was then that I began to think about the lack of acquisitiveness in myself that I have earlier written of. When I saw Manny's apartment, I at once understood its meaning for both of us. He lived in one large room in a loft building in Brooklyn. The room was bright and clean and neat. In it he had one bed, one table, two chairs, and a lamp; in the kitchen, two pots and a frying pan, two dinner plates, two cups, two sets of flatware, three or four drinking glasses. Minimal, I thought dryly, very minimal . . . and in that instant saw myself plain.

It was as though suddenly I had come to realize that things lend warmth and color to one's surround, give it weight, context, dimension. A world stripped of things leaves the atmosphere stark: black, white, and unpopulated. If you didn't want things the way Manny and I didn't want things, it could only mean you were willing to live with the confirmation of a sense of marginality strong enough to cause the brooding self to stand stock-still, for years on end.

There in that neat, empty room I saw this long moodiness of life in Manny, and its ineluctable consequence in me. Remarkably, I felt affection for the me I saw reflected in Manny's stripped-down space. Standing there in its doorway, I felt my heart go out to him. I embraced him, I closed with him.

But mutual disability is an unreliable magnet. The moment always comes when it repels rather than attracts.

Within the year it became clear that love would bring us neither peace nor stability. Nostalgia and chemistry had brought us together and were keeping us together, but the incursions on pleasure being made by needs that originate in places other than the senses began rapidly to multiply. The most vital form of connection other than sex is conversation. It was important to both Manny and me to speak, and to be heard, but within months we seemed to disagree on almost everything—and disagreement was invariably perceived as repudiation. The simplest difference in opinion became a matter for dispute; and a conversation of any substance established a failure of connection that all too often proved near fatal. Repeatedly, we startled ourselves with the quickly flaring temper that began to characterize almost every exchange. The volatility was astonishing: it leaped ahead like brushfire, and within seconds we were going down in flames.

For my part, I passed many an hour trying to retrace the course of these conversational disasters, wondering which was the sentence offered as a stimulation that had been received as a challenge, the response that had scattered my insights, the nuance that had flattened his. Why, I wondered as I sat alone late at night, did we come so close, yet remain apart? We were both decent, intelligent, literate. We both pulled the same lever in the voting booth, read the same book reviews in the *Times*. Neither of us was in real estate or city government. What was going wrong here? The answer to these questions was always the same.

Good conversation is not a matter of mutuality of interests or class concerns or commonly held ideals, it's a matter of temperament: the thing that makes someone respond instinctively with an appreciative "I know just what you mean," rather than the argumentative "Whaddaya mean by that?" In the presence of shared temperament, conversation almost never loses its free, unguarded flow; in its absence, one is always walking on eggshells.

In the heat of our quarrels, I inevitably tried to calm myself by observing, "Look, we're just not on each other's wavelength, that's all, different wavelengths." I spoke these words as though I thought them a neutral evaluation of our problem, but Manny always heard them as a put-down, even though they were as true for him as they were for me. Yet it was also true, what those words meant, when I spoke them, was that in his presence my own mind became a burden to me. I grew defensive when made to explain what I should have been allowed to explore, felt closed off and then shut down.

The irony was that the worse the quarrels became between me and Manny, the more I dreaded losing him. Within six months of our having been together, I had become terminally thin-skinned, making one scene after another because I could not control the feeling that I no longer had all of his sexual attention. In bed I knew he adored me, yet it seemed to me that he was eyeing every pretty woman in the street, that I no longer looked as sufficiently good to him as I once had. Now, his every word, every gesture, every flick of the eyes, was continually being measured against an invisible ruler marked "He loves me more today than he did yesterday, less than he did an hour ago, not as much as two weeks ago."

The thing was, we weren't friends. Without friendship, we were each alone in the wilderness.

I began to realize what everyone in the world knows and routinely forgets: that to be loved sexually is to be loved not for one's actual self but for one's ability to arouse desire in the other. It was a given that the powers assigned the me that Manny desired would be short-lived. Only the thoughts in one's mind or intuitions of the spirit can attract permanently, and those in mine Manny did not love. He did not hate them, but neither did he love them. They were not necessary to him. Ultimately, this connection of the senses meant that I would be thrown back on myself to an intolerable degree, made to feel so vulnerable that I was soon drowning in self-doubt.

I once asked Manny if he was surprised at how his life had turned out. He said to me, "I've always felt pulled around by forces beyond my control. I'd do what people expected of me, and then I'd get anxious. For years I knew no condition but anxiety. One day I realized the anxiety had formed me. After that there were no surprises."

At the end of one incendiary exchange, I flung myself on Manny's neck. For one long moment I hung there, like dead weight. Then his arms closed around me. He smoothed my hair back with a gesture of such exquisite tenderness, I can feel it to this day. He knew that we were cashing out. Very soon now, there would be no currency left with which to buy time.

•

Leonard and I, having bought the makings of a dinner we are preparing together, are standing in line in the supermarket when an old woman, thin and trembling, already at the checker's register, realizes she's forgotten something. Her eyes begin to roll in her head—oh God, she'll lose her place in the line! The high school student standing right behind her puts his hand on the old woman's arm and asks what it is she's forgotten. Milk, comes the answer. Leonard emits a sound of unmistakable exasperation. The student runs quick and gets the milk. The old woman says, "Oh, you are so kind, so kind, so extraordinarily kind!" The student says, "No, only

moderately kind." I beam at him—a soul mate!—
but Leonard says to him, "Now, that's an interesting distinction. Considering the circumstance, your
action might seem extraordinary rather than ordinary. In New York, to go out of your way to help
someone is to interrupt conventional inconvenience;
delay, deflect, detain; stop the action; pursue reflec-
tion." The student stares at him. "In short," Leonard explains, "risk assault."

What I never feel in the city he feels every day of
his life.

•

They met in Florence in 1880. He was thirty-seven,
she forty. She was Constance Fenimore Woolson, a
popular American writer of essays and stories—
and he? He was Henry James. To his great surprise,
he saw quickly that she was a woman of taste and
judgment whose self-divisions mirrored his own.
She enjoyed reputation but burrowed into obscurity; she feared loneliness yet courted solitude; she
wished to be openhearted yet came off as evasive.
Once, when James was considering taking a flat in
Venice, Constance said to him, "I don't imagine you
on the Grand Canal," and he replied: "No. Somewhere hidden. It does not matter quite where, as
long as it is difficult to find, with many blind alleys
on the way." He was speaking for her as well as

himself. From earliest youth, she'd begun building her armor of defensive reserve; by the time she came of age it was in place; by the time she died it was suffocating her.

They walked and they talked; they took tea and they talked; they went to museums and they talked. They talked books, they talked writing, they talked the moral imagination. The exchange was, of course, not personal in any usual sense, but the intellectual honesty that animated their talk resulted in a conversation that made each of them feel less alone in the world.

Without question she gave him more than he gave her. She became his best reader, his most intelligent interlocutor, the one more than any other who understood all in life that went unspoken and unsaid. The same could not be said for James, who took flagrant advantage of all between them that went unspoken and unsaid. He seems, almost willfully, never to have grasped the depth of her anguish; or, if he did, he chose, with a hand shading his eyes, not to look directly into it. Perhaps it was that he knew if he did let that information penetrate him, he'd be forced to become more accountable to the friendship. Above all else, Henry James feared and hated being held accountable.

In the spring of 1893, Constance—now deep into one of her serious depressions—occupies a flat in a palazzo fronting the Grand Canal. Henry is delighted and promises to come to Venice in the winter. She writes immediately to say the prospect of his visit is elating. No sooner does he get this letter than his anxieties begin to rise. In midsummer he writes to say he's working on a new book, his plans for the winter are unsettled, it is more than likely that he will not come to Venice at all. She is silent. The summer drifts by, and then the autumn, with hardly a communiqué passing between them. Then comes a letter from Constance casually announcing that the novel she's been working on is finished. He knows that when she is between writing projects she rapidly starts to sink, but somehow the information does not register. He lets things ride.

In January 1894, Constance Woolson jumped from a window in her Venetian flat, spattering her incredibly stripped-down life on a pavement washed by the waters of the most glamorous seaway in the world. After her death, the American diplomat John Hay said of her, "She had not as much happiness as a convict." James, at home in England, felt horror, panic, guilt: whether or not he felt pain is not known. Somewhere within himself, he must have thought, If I'd gone to Venice, she wouldn't have jumped.

The truth of the matter is that neither Woolson nor James was equal to the task of friendship. While both cherished the connection, more compelling by far was the neurotic unhappiness within which each was imprisoned. Neither could do for the other what they could not do for themselves.

•

The night after I'd read about Woolson and James, I became a literary groupie. I dreamed that Leonard and I had both given up our own apartments in order to live together, and now, in the dream, he had called to say he'd found a place for us on the Upper East Side, where, in waking reality, neither of us would ever live. Quick, he says on the phone, come see it. I run uptown, enter a classy-looking building, push open the apartment door, and I am standing in a room, long and narrow, that feels like a coffin. At the far end of the room is a curtained window. I rush to it, thinking, The view will make up for it. I tear the curtain aside and I am staring at a brick wall.

•

I stepped onto the Number 3 bus on Fifth Avenue at Sixty-Sixth Street just as the afternoon rush hour was beginning. The seat near the door directly opposite the driver was empty, and I dropped into it. At Fifty-Ninth Street the bus began to fill up. As people crowded on, my eyes watched hand after hand drop and retrieve the MetroCard from the fare box and then move past my fixed gaze. At Fifty-

Third Street someone got on without making the automatic gesture toward the box. I looked up and saw that it was an old man settling himself heavily in the seat diagonally opposite me.

The bus went one more stop. Then the driver turned in his seat and said, "Sir, you didn't pay your fare." The old man didn't answer; he was staring at the floor, his hands resting lightly on the head of a walking stick planted between his knees.

The driver repeated himself.

The old man looked up. "Yes, I did," he said.

The driver stared at him. "No, sir," he said patiently, "you did not pay your fare."

"Yes, I did," the old man said, and went back to staring at the floor.

At the next light the driver swung out of his seat and stood before the old man. "Sir," he said, "I can't go on until you pay your fare."

The old man looked up. "I paid the fare," he said evenly. "I can't help it if you didn't see me do it. I'm not going to do it twice."

The old man and the driver locked eyes. Slowly, the stare became a glare. The old man began to look like a bulldog, the driver another kind of animal. The old man was white, the driver was black; for a moment I thought . . .

"Mister," the driver yelled, "this bus ain't going nowhere until you pay your fare."

"Omigod," the woman beside me breathed.

"What the hell is going on?" a man three seats down called out.

"I paid," the old man said again.

"He's paid, all right," a man said softly.

The driver switched off the ignition and began speaking into the phone on his dashboard. Up and down the aisle people perked up with interest and agitation.

A woman in black leaned toward a man wearing horn-rimmed glasses and, one finger tapping the side of her forehead, stage-whispered, "Senile."

"Hey," a voice called out from the back. "Let's get this show on the road, I gotta get downtown."

Two people began discussing the legal and social ramifications of the case. "Ain't no way that driver-man can keep goin', he don't pay the fare," said one. "But what if the old man ain't got the money?" said the other. "Baby, you ain't got no money, you don't get on no bus," came the swift reply. "That's the law, man, the law."

The driver stood in the aisle and announced loudly, "Everybody off the bus. Sorry, folks, but this bus is not moving. I'll give you all transfers."

Stunned silence. Nobody could believe this was happening. Then everyone was yelling at once: "What the hell, I gotta get, you can't do this to us."

At the back of the bus, a wounded howl went

up from a young man who until this moment had been dreaming out the window. Now he stood up, his slim body a glory of black leather and silver studs. He stalked to the front of the bus, planted himself before the silent old man, and spat out, "What-choo wanna make yourself so *cheap* for? For a lousy buck and a quarter. Man, for that you gonna put us through all this misery?"

The driver, a tall, well-built man, stood unmoving as the passengers streamed toward the doors, but in his face I thought I saw an accumulation of the insults that daily life flung at him. In thirty seconds we were all off the bus, milling about in the street. Interestingly enough, no one walked away and no one speculated on why not one of us had thought to simply pay the old man's fare.

"Oh, this lousy city," the man beside me crooned softly, "goddamn this lousy city."

I looked back at the bus. The old man was still sitting in his seat, his hands on his walking stick, his eyes on the floor. Suddenly, as the confusion on the street was mounting, he stood up, climbed off the bus, and, like a figure in a dream, walked away into the crowded afternoon. I plucked at the driver's sleeve. "He's gone," I said.

The driver's glance followed mine, and without the flick of an eyelash, he announced, "Okay, everybody back on the bus."

In silence, everyone filed back onto the bus.
Each passenger sat down in the same seat he or she
had occupied before. The driver took his seat,
closed the doors, and swung expertly out into Fifth
Avenue traffic. I looked at my watch. One hour had
elapsed from the time the driver had first said, "Sir,
you didn't pay your fare." I looked around at my
fellow travelers and saw that each had quickly rear-
ranged his or her face behind its compulsory mask
of neutrality. It was as though, for them, nothing
had ever happened. But even then I knew better.

·

In the early 1950s, a New York journalist named
Seymour Krim yearned to be a maker of dissident
literature at the same time that he wished to enjoy
national celebrity—and on both scores felt himself
a failure. Out of that sense of failure, Krim found a
voice and a subject that spoke to the times. His per-
sona was that of a manic-depressive, alternately
ambitious, neurotic, self-mocking, and it spilled
rivers of ink delivering an ongoing account of its
breakdowns, its hungers, its shocking envy of those
who had achieved the success that was both de-
spised and longed for. That voice was also urban to
the core. No place on earth other than New York
City could have produced a Seymour Krim.

Making provocative use of a mad, inventive,

somewhat stream-of-consciousness sentence structure, Krim developed a hipster prose style that allowed him, in spirit, to join a generation of emerging rebels for whom thought, feeling, and action were about to become one. For Krim, achieving such unity would mean bringing his own inner chaos under sufficient control that he'd be able to write the great work he *knew* he had it in him to write.

Fantasy was his middle name. He was forever fantasizing a future in which all would be magically pulled together and—of this he was certain—his own big time promise would blossom into major accomplishment. The fantasizing saturated nearly every piece he ever wrote. A nervous braggadocio beneath the surface of the prose made his narrator sound as though he imagined himself the protagonist in a Broadway musical, calling out to the audience, "Just you wait and see! I'm gonna come out of this bigger, better, more important than ALL OF YOU PUT TOGETHER."

But consolidation of thought and action remained beyond Krim's grasp. All he could do was document the disability that tore him up every day that he awakened in the cold-water flat on the Lower East Side that he lived in until he died. At the height of his powers, Krim's gift was to speak for all those like him who were also unable to convert fantasy into reality. Through the simple expedient of using this defiantly daydreaming self as an instrument of illumination, Krim sought to make a metaphor of the American inability to grow up and get down to work.

Too often Krim's anxiety swamped the metaphor, and when it did the writing was reduced to a disheveled rant, tiresome and pathetic. In 1973, however, he wrote "For My Brothers and Sisters in the Failure Business," a remarkable essay in which he at long last *did* pull together the subject he had spent years making his own. Here, he was able to capture brilliantly the American obsession with failure itself—the taste of it, the fear of it, the forever being haunted by it—and when he did, his message was delivered in language that made prodigious use of the New York vernacular:

"At 51," he wrote,

> believe it or not, or believe it and pity me if you are young and swift, I still don't know truly "what I want to be.". . . In that profuse upstairs delicatessen of mine I'm as open to every wild possibility as I was at 13 . . .
>
> Thousands upon thousands of people who I believe are like me are those who have never found the professional skin to fit the riot in their souls. Many never will . . . This isn't presumption so much as a voice of

scars and stars talking. I've lived it and will probably go on living it until they take away my hotdog . . .

But if you are a proud, searching "failure" in this society and we can take ironic comfort in the fact that there are hundreds of thousands of us, then it is smart and honorable to know what you attempted and why you are now vulnerable to the body blows of those who once saw you robed in the glow of your vision and now only see an unmade bed and a few unwashed cups on the bare wooden table of a gray day.

The pleasure of this piece lies in the rich, sure speed of an idiomatic language that mimics the national preoccupation with youth as well as failure:

That profuse upstairs delicatessen of mine
The riot in their souls
A voice of scars and stars
Those who only see an unmade bed and a few unwashed cups on the bare wooden table of a gray day

Idiomatic speech always feels young—in any language it makes the adrenaline shoot right up—but never more so than in the edgy, street-smart version of it one hears on the pavements of New York, where middle-aged writers of American prose are free to cry out in voices forever young, "I'm no longer young!"

•

Leonard went away for a holiday weekend without telling me he was leaving the city, and he left his answering machine off.

"What was that all about?" I asked upon his return.

"Oh," he said sheepishly, "I left the machine off accidentally." But the laugh that followed was hollow. "I guess I didn't want to know that no one was calling me."

"But someone was calling you. Me."

"Yes," he said, his voice ominously vague. "You *were*, weren't you."

•

For eight years I taught one semester a year in Arizona. Often, upon my return to the city, encounters like the following would take place:

I'd run into Eli, a writer I know. His face in repose is apprehensive, but when I ask how he is, it brightens and he tells me that he's just signed a book contract. I congratulate him, ask about the family, and then about Paul, another writer we both know. Eli sighs. His face reverts to apprehensive. "He always has to top me," he says. "If I've been invited to L.A. he's been invited to Hawaii. If I have a book coming out he's got two. If I win a CAPS he's won a Rockefeller."

Hours later I run into Gloria, an old acquaintance of mine who obsesses over financial ruin and her miserably indifferent family.

"How's it going?" I ask.

"My father?" she replies. "He says, 'Get a reverse mortgage.' My nieces and nephews? I never see them. My sister-in-law? She'd be happy to see me out on the street. And my brother? He's a pussy!"

Myra, who's often told me she thinks of me as one of her best friends, invariably looks quizzically at me, as though she can't quite place me, and asks, "Where've you been? Out in Oklahoma, someplace?"

And then there's Sylvia, a devotee of the therapeutic culture. Two years in a row she grins at me and says, "I've gotten so mature I no longer demand of my friends that they give me what they cannot give. I now accept friendship on the terms that it is offered." The third year the grin dies on her face. "I hate it!" she hisses. "It makes life feel small. Small and partial."

My friends, too, must shake the kaleidoscope of

daily experience to arrive at a composition that will help mediate the pain of intimacy, the vibrancy of public space, and the exquisite intervention of strangers.

I turn the corner onto Seventh Avenue and a very large cross-dresser is standing squarely in front of me, eyes squeezed shut, hands joined as though in prayer, calling into the air, "I have so many enemies!" When his eyes open they meet mine. "Why?" I mouth silently. He gives me a brilliant smile and announces joyously, "I don't *know*."

•

Some ten or fifteen years ago, a woman of my acquaintance (I'll call her Jane Brown) had an affair with a man who was heir to a famous American fortune (I'll call him Roger Newman). At the time of their meeting, they were both storefront lawyers serving a slum neighborhood in Brooklyn. For Jane, the work was the natural culmination of a Quaker childhood, a good education, and a devout sense of political idealism. For Roger, the work was done in defiance of unearned privilege, a proper rather than an erotic marriage, and a future in the family business that precluded the promise of purposeful employment.

Working side by side, these two had fallen in love and Roger had left his wife to move in with

Jane. Friends soon said they were living together in blissful harmony, and some were surprised when Roger began working even longer hours than he had before, his objection to the laws that thwarted his underprivileged clients having grown ever more ardent. Jane was proud of Roger's deepened sense of engagement, yet even she urged him to slow down. Roger, however, told her that never before in his life had he felt as free as he now did. To plunge into hard, meaningful work, he said, was a joy; and to have at his side a woman who shared his belief in the work an added pleasure he had never hoped to experience. They were together for two years. Then one afternoon without warning or explanation, Roger announced that he was leaving both Jane and the practice and returning to his wife and the family business. Within a matter of days he was gone.

In college my friends and I had played an Edith Wharton–Henry James game in which a story was told—invariably the setting was bourgeois New York, the moral dilemma a matter of emotional courage—and the question asked was: Who would have written this story, Wharton or James? Roger Newman's retreat to his once repudiated life had, at the time, brought the game back into my mind, and I'd always been curious to know the outcome of his action. So two weeks ago when a lawyer I know phoned to say he'd been invited to dinner at the

Newmans', would I like to come, I of course said
yes, and at seven o'clock the following Saturday evening, the lawyer and I got out of a cab in front of a
Park Avenue building at the corner of Sixty-Sixth
Street, where we were admitted to a marble-and-
onyx lobby the size of a small cathedral and entered
an oak-paneled elevator equipped with red velvet
bench seats. When we stepped off the elevator on the
nineteenth floor, we were in the Newman apartment.
Our host was as I remembered him—middling tall,
reed slim, with soft brown hair and blue eyes set in
an inconspicuously handsome face—only now, I was
struck by how well his clothes fit him and the grace
with which he wore them.

The living room was huge: Persian rugs, old English furniture, silken lamp shades. Seven men and
women sat on the furniture. The women had blond
hair and long legs, the men bore a strong resemblance to Newman himself. One of the women was
Cissy, Roger's wife. She shook my hand and said she
was glad to meet me, she'd been reading me for years.
I thanked her for having me, and we all sat down
with a drink in our hands. An hour later the whole
company rose and walked into the dining room,
where dinner was being served. The plates were gold-
rimmed china, the wineglasses thin crystal, the forks
heavy silver. The food was delicious, but there wasn't
enough of it. The wine, however, flowed.

As the tone, syntax, and vocabulary of this group were foreign to me, I did not at first grasp the banality of the conversation. People introduced subjects in order to allude, not to discuss. There'd be three minutes on the headlines, seven on European travel, two on the current exhibit at MoMA. Real estate went a good ten or fifteen minutes, as did the cost of the children's education, vacation plans, the current scandal on Wall Street. Strong opinion was clearly unwelcome, as was sustained exchange.

Roger himself—an elegant host who pulled out chairs, passed dishes, refreshed drinks with unobtrusive courtesy—played an interesting role here. He initiated nothing; on the other hand, he never expressed a foolish or an insensitive thought. If serious disagreement threatened among his guests, he made the kind of judicious comment that quickly put the contestants at their ease and short-circuited potential rupture at the dinner table. His tone of voice throughout was uniformly light, conciliatory, civilized.

Cissy Newman was a pretty woman who picked fretfully at her food and wore a thin layer of anxiety over her makeup. At one point, from out of nowhere she blurted at me, "But, after all, don't you think a child needs his mother?" I stared blankly at her. "Don't I think a child needs his mother?" I repeated idiotically. It was then that Roger laughed easily and surprised me by saying in a voice both soft and kind, "Cissy, Cissy, that's not her point," and then proceeding, with remarkable equanimity, to give a wonderfully reasoned précis of the feminist position with which he identified me. Cissy and I both sat there, nodding like a pair of grateful students who've been released by a skillful teacher from their own mental incompetence.

I remember thinking then, What is he doing here? Why has he deliberately put himself back into this life? And I began to watch him.

After dinner, I sat at one end of a brocade-covered couch, while Roger sat beside me in a velvet-covered armchair. A stream of chitchat formed itself all around us and, separately, we each joined in from time to time; but repeatedly I saw Roger's eyes rise above the faces of the company and come to rest on the larger surround. When he did, not only was his pleasure unmistakable, his satisfaction seemed profound. Clearly, the ease with which he wore his clothes extended to the ease with which he inhabited this room. As he looked about him, he absentmindedly stroked the velvet arm of his chair with an absorptiveness that made the caress of his hand seem that of a lover on the arm of the beloved. At the same time, he periodically eased his body forward in the chair to pick from the coffee table a marble egg that rested on a worked-gold stand, rolling the egg about smoothly and again lovingly in the palm of his hand, then returning it carefully to its place on the stand. When he spoke, he held his wineglass in such a way that he seemed more aware of the feel of the crystal stem between his fingers than of the words coming out of his mouth. It was as though the people in the room were figures in the foreground of a history painting, our host clearly heir to the painting.

I found myself thinking, Who or what is this reminding me of? Another minute and I had it. I was watching Ashley Wilkes, a man of developed sensibility and liberal inclination made inert by a will bound to a way of life rather than a spirit in consultation with itself.

For a moment, Roger Newman—working in the ghetto, in love with Jane Brown—had had an overpowering need to experience passion firsthand. His considerable intelligence had told him that it was a plus, as well, to know what was being said and done on those streets down below; but it had always been a given that any foray into them would be in the nature of a temporary investigation.

As the lawyer and I were walking down Park Avenue at midnight, I said to myself, Henry James would have written this story, not Edith Wharton. Wharton thought no one could *have* freedom, but James knew no one *wanted* freedom.

•

When the influence of European modernism crossed the Atlantic at the turn of the twentieth century, it made its first full stop in Greenwich Village. There, a generation of artists, intellectuals, journalists, and social theorists came together to make a revolution in consciousness. Among them were women and men whose names are now inscribed in the history books: Edna St. Vincent Millay, Alfred Stieglitz, Margaret Sanger, Eugene O'Neill, Emma Goldman, Walter Lippmann—an unlikely collection of cultural bedfellows drawn together by the spirit behind the movement. *Experience* was now king, and everyone wanted it: unimpeded sexual adventure, alarmingly bold conversation, extreme eccentricity of dress; declaring oneself free to not marry or make a living, have children or vote. These became the extravagant conventions of downtown radicalism—and none adhered more strictly to them than Evelyn Scott, a writer of the 1920s whose name was once known to every Village modernist. Thirty years later, Scott was living with her husband, an alcoholic English writer, in a boarding-house on Manhattan's Upper West Side; both of them now old, ill, half-mad, and almost wholly destitute.

In 1963, Evelyn died and the English husband,

through the intervention of old friends, was repatriated back to London, where he died a few years later, in an alcoholic stupor, in pretty much the same boardinghouse as the one Evelyn had died in in New York. His remains were a collection of shopping bags, small suitcases, a trunk or two. These were hauled off to a book and antiques shop in the Camden district of London, where they gathered dust for a decade and more. Then they were shipped off to a junk shop in Yorkshire. There, one day in the late seventies, an amateur book dealer, a man of literary taste, opened one of the trunks and came across a collection of Evelyn Scott's letters, diaries, and novels (both published and in manuscript). He began reading. At first mystified, he was soon absorbed. Who was this woman? How had she come to write these books? Why had he never heard of her?

The book dealer (his name was D. A. Callard) spent the next five years, on both sides of the Atlantic, trying to answer these questions. The fruit of his labor was a biography, published in 1985 and called *Pretty Good for a Woman* (a crack made by William Faulkner about Scott's work) When the book was published in the United States, a friend came over, tossed it on my coffee table, and said, "This is your cup of tea." And so it was.

She was born Elsie Dunn in Tennessee in 1893.

From earliest childhood she was experienced as wild, literary, sexual. In 1913 at the age of twenty she ran away to Brazil with a forty-four-year-old married university dean. Here, the odd couple renamed themselves Evelyn and Cyril Scott. They lived together for years, ran about the world, had a child, shared every outlier view going. From this relationship Evelyn emerged determined on an outrageous life.

In Brazil she began sending stories and poems to the little magazines back home. She had a talent for the ideas and syntax of Imagism; her work was accepted; her name began to be known. By the time she arrived in Greenwich Village in 1919, she was connected. Within thirty seconds she knew every writer and painter in the neighborhood, and they all knew her.

In the Village the air itself was filled with anarchism, Freudianism, sexual radicalism. Evelyn embraced it all: violently. She began writing for the *Dial*, the *Egoist*, the *Little Review*. She championed Joyce and Lawrence, published poetry of her own and then novels and criticism in a fairly steady stream over the next fifteen years. All in all she wrote a dozen novels, two volumes of poetry, two memoirs, and a play. Her writing was alternately brilliant and unreadable—sometimes composed in the style of stream of consciousness, sometimes that of German expressionism, sometimes that of Dos

Passos modernism. In whichever style, the writing was over-the-top. The word *megalomania* appears in more than one review of a Scott novel. It might also have been applied to her personality, marked as it was by fantasies of its own high-minded purity and its demands that others be as nakedly honest in life and art as she was. In his memoir Cyril Scott said of her, "The only mark of 'goodness' [that she recognized] was complete lack of reticence. This she called 'honesty' . . . and broke with whoever objected."

She took lovers easily and frequently, among them the critic Waldo Frank, the poet William Carlos Williams, and the painter Owen Merton, father of Thomas Merton. Williams met her when she was twenty-seven. He thought she had a talent that would mature. Very quickly he changed his mind. He found her a woman of extraordinary willfulness who demanded surrender, both in her relationships and in her prose. The willfulness, as it turned out, prefigured a capacity for obsession that would eventually morph into full-blown paranoia.

Yet she was exciting and memorable. A remarkable group of people—including Emma Goldman, Kay Boyle, Caroline Gordon—remained attached to her, touched as they were by the brilliance and the madness, the driving hunger that had found release in bohemianism but could not be disciplined to better the work.

When the 1920s came to a close, an entire generation of artists suddenly found its work un-
wanted. Overnight, lyrical modernism had given
way to social realism, and Evelyn Scott's writing
(along with the writing of many others) was a thing
of the past. No longer able to get her work published,
she became seriously disoriented. An acute sense of
persecution developed and, convinced that the Com-
munists were plotting against her, she began writing
continuously of the Red menace: in print, in private
correspondence, and finally in letters to the FBI.

The years passed and soon she and her husband
were scraping by in that boardinghouse room on
the Upper West Side. Sometime in the late fifties,
the poet and critic Louise Bogan ran into Evelyn on
Broadway and later wrote of the encounter in a letter to her friend May Sarton:

> I had a sad and rather eerie meeting, early
> this week, with poor old Evelyn Scott . . .
> frayed and dingy and more than a little
> mad . . . She is not only in the physical state
> I [myself] once feared, but she is living in the
> blighted area of the West 70s, that area which
> absorbs the queer, the old, the failures, into
> furnished or hotel rooms, and adds gloom to
> their decay. It was all there! She took me to a
> grubby little tea room, insisted on paying

for the tea, and brought out from time to time, from folds of her apparel, manuscripts that will never see print. I never *was* able to read her, even in her hey-day, and her poetry now is perfectly terrible. Added to all this she is in an active state of paranoia—things and people are her enemies; she has been plotted against in Canada, Hampstead, New York, and California; her manuscripts have been stolen time and again, etc. etc. As you know I really fear mad people; I have some attraction for them because talent is a kind of obverse of the medal. I must, therefore, detach myself from E.S. I told her to send the MS to Grove Press, and that is all I can do.

The two women parted on Broadway, one turning north, the other south. They'd each taken only a few steps when Evelyn looked back and cried out, "But I must know the editor's name! I can't chance having my poems fall into the hands of some secretary!"

Imagine: I might have been just around the corner on West End Avenue, a college girl daydreaming herself into a writing life at the very moment that Evelyn Scott was crying out, "I must know the editor's name!"

•

In a student coffee shop near NYU, two young women are talking.

"Guess what?" one says. "I saw *Romeo and Juliet* on Broadway last week."

"Oh, yeah?" the other says. "Is that thing modern?"

A frown creases the forehead of the theatergoer before she says, "The setting is modern, the language is old. But it works."

In a booth across the aisle, two young men sit reading.

"Guess what?" one says.

The other one looks up from his book.

"Flaubert's mother wrote him a letter in which she said, 'Your mania for sentences has dried up your heart.'"

The same frown creases the forehead of the respondent before he says, "Meaning?"

•

For many years I walked six miles a day. I walked to clear my head, experience street life, dispel afternoon depression. During those walks I daydreamed incessantly. Sometimes I daydreamed the past—idealizing remembered moments of love or praise—but mostly I daydreamed the future: the tomorrow in which I would write a book of enduring value, meet the companion of my life, become the woman of character I had yet to become. Ah, that tomor-row! How wonderfully its energetic projections got me through innumerable days of wasteful passivity. Not unlike Seymour Krim, I never tired of imagin-ing new scenarios for my daydreaming life as I tramped the streets and boulevards that many years of steady walking covered. Then, just as I was turn-ing sixty, an unusual development sent this cozy setup into a tailspin.

That spring I was teaching in Arizona and walk-ing daily along a road at the edge of the town, taking new pleasure in the physical beauty that surrounded me (the mountains, the desert, the clarity of light), but, as usual, running a movie in my head. One after-noon in April, right in the middle of the film, a kind of visual static—something like the static on a tele-vision screen—cut across my inner field of vision; the "story" began literally to break up before my eyes and then it actually terminated itself. At the same time an acrid taste began to fill my mouth and, deep within, I felt myself shrinking from: I knew not what.

The entire incident was so strange, so baffling, that it mystified rather than alarmed me, and I thought to myself, An aberrant occurrence, expect no repeats. But the next day exactly the same thing happened. There I was, walking along the black-topped road, another movie under way in my head, when again: the story short-circuited itself, the acrid taste filled my mouth, and again I felt myself blanching before some unnameable anxiety. When on the third day the entire process repeated itself, it became clear that a sea change was in progress.

Before long I became sufficiently gun-shy—I had begun to dread the nastiness in my mouth—to want to suppress the daydreaming; and lo and behold, it turned out that I could. Now, no sooner did the images start to form in my head than I found myself able to wipe them clean before they could take hold. It was then that the really strange and interesting thing happened. A vast emptiness began to open up behind my eyes as I went about my daily business. The daydreaming, it seemed, had occupied more space than I'd ever imagined. It was as though the majority of my waking time had routinely been taken up with fantasizing, only a narrow portion of consciousness concentrated on the here and now. Of this I was convinced, because of the number of times a day the bitter taste threatened to take up residence in my mouth.

The insight was stunning. I began to realize what daydreaming had done for me—and to me.

Ever since I could remember, I had feared being found wanting. If I did the work I wanted to do, it was certain not to measure up; if I pursued the people I wanted to know, I was bound to be rejected; if I made myself as attractive as I could, I would still

be ordinary looking. Around such damages to the
ego a shrinking psyche had formed itself: I applied
myself to my work, but only grudgingly; I'd make
one move toward people I liked, but never two; I
wore makeup but dressed badly. To do any or all of
these things well would have been to engage heed-
lessly with life—love it more than I loved my fears—
and this I could not do. What I could do, apparently,
was daydream the years away: go on yearning for
"things" to be different so that I would be different.

Turning sixty was like being told I had six
months to live. Overnight, retreating into the refuge
of a fantasized tomorrow became a thing of the
past. Now there was only the immensity of the va-
cated present. Then and there I vowed to take seriously the task of filling it. But, of course, easier said
than done. It wasn't hard to cut short the daydreaming, but how exactly did one manage to occupy the
present when for so many years one hadn't? Days
passed, then weeks and months in which I dreaded
waking into my own troubled head. I thought often
in those days of Virginia Woolf's phrase *moments
of being*—because I wasn't having any.

Then—seemingly from one day to the next I
became aware, after one of my street encounters,
that the vacancy within was stirring with movement. A week later another encounter left me feeling curiously enlivened. It was the third one that did

it. A hilarious exchange had taken place between me and a pizza deliveryman, and sentences from it now started repeating themselves in my head as I walked on, making me laugh each time anew, and each time with yet deeper satisfaction. Energy—coarse and rich—began to swell inside the cavity of my chest. Time quickened, the air glowed, the colors of the day grew vivid; my mouth felt fresh. A surprising tenderness pressed against my heart with such strength it seemed very nearly like joy; and with unexpected sharpness I became alert not to the meaning but to the astonishment of human existence. It was there on the street, I realized, that I was filling my skin, occupying the present.

•

"I don't like male energy. Too hard, too forward, too direct. It's not really interesting. The gestures, the motions, the whole repertoire. Too limited. Not like with women. No nuance, no modulation. It's not *attractive*. And then sometimes it's suffocating."

I've heard many women speak these words or words much like them. This time, however, it was Leonard who was speaking them.

•

Release from the wounds of childhood is a task never completed, not even on the point of death. A friend of mine, dying of cancer, was still locked into a power struggle with a husband who had failed to provide her with a marriage that compensated for what she had suffered at the hands of her own brutish family. Although this husband had been consistently faithful—and a trouper throughout her long, terrible illness—my friend had never trusted him any more than she had her philandering father. One day when she was weeks from death, the husband asked me to spell him while he made an overnight visit to some friends in the country. Next morning, no sooner had I taken his place at her bedside than my friend clutched my arm and croaked at me, "I think Mike has another woman." I stared wordlessly at her. "I won't stand for it!" she cried. "I want a divorce."

It's five o'clock on a Saturday afternoon in summer, and my mother and I are walking on the avenue that fronts the Manhattan housing project where she lives. The sun is blazing down on the usual: sirens screeching, car horns honking, Con Ed drilling, while three Hispanics have an argument, two gay women embrace, an addict slides down a storefront window. Neither of us pays them any attention, especially not my mother, who is relating a tale of grievance to me. In one sense, this neighborhood has made a New Yorker of my mother; in another, she has remained the stubbornly life-offended woman she has been nearly all the years I have known her.

We run into Mara, a neighbor who's usually seen walking with her husband. Now, here she is on her own, on her way to a six o'clock movie. We stand talking for a moment or two, then go our separate ways.

"It's Saturday night," my mother says, "she's walking around alone?" Her voice drips insinuation.

"It's five in the afternoon," I say.

"By the time she gets out of the movie it will be night," she says.

I shrug.

"Maybe her husband's out of town," I say.

"Why, he's a salesman?" she says.

A few blocks on we run into Mrs. Grossman, another neighbor from the project. This woman is well dressed, carefully made up, eighty years old if she's a day.

"Tell me," she says to my mother, "is it true Lionel Levine is dead?"

"Yes," my mother says drily, "he's dead."

"Did he die alone?"

"Yes, he died alone."

"Tell me," Mrs. G says, her voice now smarmy, "was he a *nice* man?"

"No," my mother says flatly. "He wasn't a nice man."

"Oh . . ." Mrs. G clucks insincerely. "That's too bad. Really, that's too bad."

Barely out of earshot my mother says, "Everybody hates her."

Now comes Boris, an old lefty shaking his fist at us while still half a block away.

"Those fuckers!" he cries. "Did you hear what those fuckers in Washington have done now?"

"No, Boris," my mother calls out, "I haven't heard. What have those fuckers in Washington done now?" Her eyes narrow. "By him," she says to me before he reaches us, "it's forever 1948."

I look silently at her. She tilts her head back, staring me down.

"Okay, okay," she says. "I know what you're thinking."

I remain silent.

One more block and she bursts out, "I can't help it! These people!"

"Still not the right ones, eh, Ma?"

•

Two Russian girls on Thirty-Fourth Street.
One stamps her feet. *"Nyet Grisha!"*
Mentally, I stamp mine. "Not George!"

•

There's a famous photograph of Robert Capa's that has been pinned to the bulletin board above my desk for a number of years. It was taken in 1948 on a beach in France, and it shows a smiling young woman dressed in a cotton gown and a large straw hat striding forward across the sands while a sturdy-looking old man walks behind her, holding a huge umbrella over her head: a queen and her slave. The young woman is Françoise Gilot and the old man Pablo Picasso. As Robert Capa was an artist, the picture is charged with emotional complexity. At first all the viewer registers is the lit-from-within triumph in Gilot's smile; and right behind it Picasso's amiable servitude. But keep looking and you'll see in Gilot's eyes that she believes her power ever-lasting; and then you'll see the cold worldliness behind Picasso's playacting deference. It hits you full force: Gilot is Anne Boleyn in her moment of glory and Picasso the appetite-driven king before he's had his fill of her.

The photograph is so richly alive, it is actually shocking: it both excites and appalls. Most days I don't even glance in its direction, but on the days that I do take it in, it never fails to arouse pain and pleasure, in equal parts. It's the equal parts that's the problem.

•

Daniel called to tell me that Tomas has cancer. I hadn't seen or heard from Tomas in three or four years, but the news knocked the wind out of me.

We'd all grown up together, in that neighborhood in the Bronx, a band of ten or fifteen children destined to keep one another company from grade school through college. Once our lives began to take shape most us had fallen away from one another, but we'd kept track over the years, as this group contained the people who had given each of us our first erotic thrill, our first experience of friendship cherished and betrayed, our first taste of privilege mysteriously extended and just as mysteriously withdrawn. Tomas was special in this group: he was the one who supplied the first hint of existential anxiety.

He had come among us when we were all about twelve years old: an orphan and a foreigner. He'd been born and raised in Italy, and when his parents died in a car crash somewhere in Europe, he'd been sent to the States, like a package, to the family of an aunt who lived in the apartment house next to ours. One day he appeared on the block—dark, silent, serious—standing calmly at the edge of a group of the boys playing ball in the middle of the street: watching, simply watching. The next day there he was again, and the day after that: dark, serious, silent. Years later he'd tell me that he'd been silent because he could hardly speak English; but even after he learned English we continued to experience him as a boy whose eerie quiet was oddly affecting:

every one of us developed the same strong urge to get a rise out of him.

The children of working-class immigrants who had neither the time nor the inclination to pay us the attention that was needed, out in the street we were wild to feel ourselves in the responses we could evoke in one another. Our games were not really games, they were exercises in which strength, smarts, cunning, ingenuity, daily determined where each of us stood in the hierarchy of value and respect in the only society that mattered: that of the kids on the block. From all this Tomas stood apart. Like everyone else, he came out on the street every day after school, but he never joined in the ball playing or the word games or the quarreling, just stood on the pavement, watching. When one of us spoke to him, as one of us regularly did, he replied monosyllabically.

Ordinarily, such a kid would either be ignored or openly rejected, but, paradoxically, the distance Tomas kept drew us to him like a magnet. There was some strange allure in his remoteness. Not one of us could have told you why, but to make Tomas respond to us was a goal we, boys and girls alike, each felt compelled to reach. Somehow, his behavior implied judgment: as though we were being appraised and found wanting. Unconsciously, I now think, every kid began to feel that if he or she had been better, smarter, more interesting, displayed more character or backbone, Tomas would happily have joined us, but as we weren't and we didn't, he chose to remain separate.

When we got older—were teenagers hanging out on the block, in the candy store, or in hallways when the weather was bad—it was the same. By now our games consisted mainly of hours-long, impassioned arguments in which at least two of us took an oppositional stand and everyone else jumped in tumultuously on one side or the other. Everyone except Tomas, who still stood among but apart from us; and whose approval we each still yearned for. In the midst of all the arguing, one or another of us would regularly turn to him to say, "Whaddaya think, Tomas?" or, "That's right, isn't it, Tomas?" Tomas in turn would now either shake his head glumly, as though to say, "Jeez, I can't believe you people," or nod slowly, as if delivering a reluctant sanction.

More than once, however, when the talk grew hotly insulting—as it did when our meager intellectual powers began to fail—Tomas would surprise us by weighing in, not on any particular element of the argument, but on our verbal savagery. He never took a position or defended an opinion, but his forehead would crease up, his mouth would start working, and then, looking puzzled himself, he'd

pronounce softly, "This ain't right, it just ain't right."
When that happened—although no one could have
told you why—the adversarial voices died down,
and we each took new stock of the situation. That's
how Tomas became our Solomon: the arbiter of
moral rightness. The more we acted out and he did
not, the more we turned to him for mediation when
the argument got out of hand; the more we turned
to him, the more anxious we each grew that his
judgment rule in our favor. And all this because he
never had a dog in the race.

For women, Tomas soon proved irresistible—
although he never had a dog in that race, either. From
the moment he turned eighteen, girls and women
swarmed around him, all of whom he treated with
the utmost courtesy whether he slept with them or
not; each of whom was convinced, at least for a
time, that she would provide the exception that
proved the rule; none of whom made a dent in his
detachment.

I don't know when it occurred to me that Tomas's
experience of early loss—parents, language, even
homeland—didn't seem a sufficient explanation
for why he was as he was; rather, it began to seem
that these losses were the objective correlative to a
condition whose origins lay elsewhere. Then one
day I realized that the distance he kept was not from
us, it was from himself, its character determined in

the absolute long ago and far away, and I remember thinking then (as I think now) that Tomas was one of those people destined almost from birth to remain a stranger to himself.

What we were witnessing as children was our first glimpse of the kind of inner remoteness that, in later life, one recognizes as primal in its very nature. In the years that followed life in the Bronx, I and nearly every woman I knew fell in love at least once with a Tomas, in each case in the same vain hope that *ours* would be the warmth that penetrated the cold at the center; vain because no amount of love can defeat the tsunami force of that primitive melancholia.

None of this could we have understood as children, but all of it we had sensed and, quite properly, experienced as a threat to our own humanity. As we had all come from sturdy peasant stock—much of it of the superstition-prone variety—it was quite remarkable that we had struggled to survive the threat by seducing it rather than beating it off with a stick.

Once, in our forties, Tomas said to me, "I've always had a funny effect on people. Like there's something in me they want to get at, some secret they think I'm keeping from them. I've never known what it's all about. I've tried to tell them, especially the women, Hey, babe, what you see is what I got. That's all there is. They don't believe me. They always think there's something more. But there ain't. Believe me. There *ain't*."

I did believe him, and I tried to explain not only his effect on us as children, but how it had taken me half a lifetime to understand it—and then, I said, it was only because as the years passed I'd often glimpsed that dangerous disconnect at work in myself. Poor beast, he didn't know what on earth I was talking about. He stood there staring at me as of old.

•

Early on a Friday evening in spring, cars coming from three directions are halted in the middle of Abingdon Square, in their midst a rat running frantically back and forth. A man turns the corner nearest to where I am standing, mesmerized. He is in his forties, wearing khaki shorts and a bright blue camp shirt and carrying a Whole Foods shopping bag in each hand. His brown thatch is graying, his features painfully delicate; his eyes blink worriedly behind designer glasses.

"What is it?" he cries at me.

His eyes follow my pointing finger.

"Oh," he says wearily. "A neur-rotic rat."

"Or else a prelude to the plague," I say.

"Now there's an only slightly more comforting thought."

For a moment the man looks thoughtful. Then he shakes his head no.

"Poor thing. He's looking for a way out and there isn't any. Believe me. I know."

He shoulders his fancy provisions anew and goes his way, now burdened by the useless wisdom he only rarely has to face up to.

•

Wandering aimlessly in the Metropolitan Museum, I find myself in the Egyptian section. It's a holiday season—what on earth impelled me to come here today?—and the place is packed with tourists: each glass case is surrounded by men, women, and children standing two feet deep, carrying these dreadful tape-recorded capsules of culture whose ear wires emit a sinister whir of noise to all within ten feet of them. At this moment I hate democracy.

But then the waves part and I am standing before a small statue of wood covered in gold leaf, with kohl-rimmed eyes painted on the gold. It is the image of a young goddess (Selket is her name) whose task it was to guard the intestines that had been scooped out of Tut's mummified body and placed in a tiny gold coffin made in his own image. She (the goddess) is stunningly beautiful, her breasts, shoulders, and stomach rounds of carved tenderness. She stands with her slim arms outstretched, as though beseeching the darkness Tut is entering to let the purity of spirit placed in her human frailty intercede for him. Unexpectedly, she moves me so deeply that the noise around me drops away, and in the sudden silence I feel tears welling up not in my eyes but from somewhere deeper down.

Although I am alone with the goddess, have no one to whom I could utter a sound, I nonetheless feel speechless: cannot find the words inside me to describe the engulfing emotion this little bit of wood and gold leaf has aroused. An awful gloom falls on me. Once again, as it has with irregular regularity throughout my waking life, that sickening sense of language buried deep within comes coursing through arms, legs, chest, throat. If only I could make it reach the brain, the conversation with myself might perhaps begin.

•

Coming downtown at midnight on Ninth Avenue, just past Fifty-Seventh Street, the bus slows up for traffic (it never ends in New York), and in the doorway of a White Rose bar stands a couple. They have their backs to the bus, but I can see they are both derelict and both reeling. The man has the woman by the arm and is pulling on it as she fumbles to open the door of the bar. Unable to shake him, she turns back to the man, and I can see her beat-up face as she mouths, "Whaddaya want from me?" He, I think, doesn't answer, just keeps pawing her. I see that hand raking ineffectually at the woman, and I can feel the despair in the rigid set of his neck. "I don' know what I want," it says, "but I *want*."

I think, Don't you two know you've got to be more attractive than you are to be playing this scene?

No. They don't know.

•

I ran into Gerald in midtown.

"You used me!" he cried.

"Not nearly well enough," I said.

He stood there looking at me, memory clouding his eyes.

"What was that all about anyway?" he asked wearily.

"Sweetheart," I said, "it could never have worked. I was headed for . . . where I am now."

"What *is* it with you?" he countered. "Why did you make such a holocaust with us? Why did you keep making scenes until all I had left was the taste in my mouth of your unholy dissatisfaction?"

I felt my eyes turning inward, toward that thick white opacity that surrounds my heart when it comes to erotic love.

"I can't do men," I said.

"What the hell does that mean," he said.

"I'm not sure."

"When *will* you be sure?"

"I don't know."

"So what do you do in the meantime?"

"Take notes."

•

The habit of loneliness persists. Leonard tells me that if I don't convert the loneliness into useful solitude, I'll be my mother's daughter forever. He is right, of course. One is lonely for the absent idealized other, but in useful solitude *I* am there, keeping myself imaginative company, breathing life into the silence, filling the room with proof of my own sentient being. It was from Edmund Gosse that I learned how to frame this insight. In his remarkable memoir, *Father and Son*, Gosse describes how at the age of eight, having discovered his father in an untruth, the child is thrown into inner turmoil. If Papa does not know everything, the child asks himself, then what *does* he know? And what is one to do with what he says? How is one to decide what to believe and what not to believe? In the midst of this confusion he suddenly realizes he's talking to himself.

"Of all the thoughts which rushed upon my savage and undeveloped little brain at this crisis,"

Gosse writes, "the most curious was that I had found a companion and a confidant in myself. There was a secret in this world and it belonged to me and to a somebody who lived in the same body with me. There were two of us, and we could talk with one another . . . It was a great solace to me to find a sympathizer in my own breast."

•

In the late nineteenth century, great books about women in modern times were written by men of literary genius. Within twenty years there had been Thomas Hardy's *Jude the Obscure*, Henry James's *The Portrait of a Lady*, George Meredith's *Diana of the Crossways*; but penetrating as these novels were, it was George Gissing's *The Odd Women* that spoke most directly to me. His were the characters I could see and hear as if they were women and men of my own acquaintance. What's more, I recognized myself as one of the "odd" women. Every fifty years from the time of the French Revolution, feminists had been described as "new" women, "free" women, "liberated" women—but Gissing had gotten it just right. We were the "odd" women.

The novel is set in London in 1887. Mary Barfoot, a gentlewoman in her fifties, is running a secretarial school to prepare middle-class girls for occupations other than that of teacher or governess. Her colleague is Rhoda Nunn, thirty years old, darkly handsome, highly intelligent, uncompromising in her open scorn for what she calls the slavery of love and marriage; there isn't an argument to be made in favor of legal union for which Rhoda doesn't have an instant comeback.

Enter Everard Barfoot, Mary's clever, well-to-do, strong-willed cousin whose intellectual sparring with Rhoda (the glory of the book) becomes steadily and mutually eroticized. The story of these two is the one that Gissing tracks with skill, patience, and understanding. What, his book asks, are men and women to be, both for themselves and for one another?

Rhoda and Everard both imagine themselves dedicated to the proposition of true partnership between the sexes, but in the final analysis, both take a two-steps-forward, one-step-back journey into self-knowledge that accounts for the snail's pace at which social change progresses.

Barfoot's intelligence persuades him that he seeks companionateness in marriage: "For him marriage must . . . mean . . . the mutual incitement of vigorous minds . . . Be a woman what else she may, let her have brains and the power of using them . . . intellect was his first requirement." Yet at the same time, an appetite for mastery exerts an even stronger pull on him. Side by side with the pleasure Rhoda's intelligence gives him, his thoughts linger on how much "a contest between his will and hers would be an amusement decidedly to his taste . . . It would delight him to enrage Rhoda and then to detain her by strength, to overcome her senses, to watch her long lashes droop over the eloquent eyes."

As for Rhoda—absolute in her conviction that women first and foremost must become "rational and responsible human beings"—she pronounces regularly on her position with a defensive bluntness that betrays her own emotional ignorance. When Barfoot chides her proud severity—"Perhaps you make too little allowance for human weakness"—she replies coldly, "Human weakness is a plea that has been much abused, and generally in an interested spirit." Everard thrills to this response, but it also makes him smile. The smile frightens Rhoda into rudeness—"Mr. Barfoot . . . if you are practicing your powers of irony, I had rather you chose some other person"—but in truth the exchange excites them both.

The attraction between them is rooted in the classical antagonism of sexual infatuation at its most compelling and its most exhausting. Bereft of tenderness or sympathy, it wears away at the nerves; consumes itself ultimately in self-division and self-regard. A year and many astonishing conversations later, when his feeling for Rhoda is considerably advanced, Barfoot is yet of two minds: "Loving her as he had never thought to love, there still remained with him so much of the temper in which he first wooed her that he could be satisfied with nothing short of unconditional surrender." Concomitantly, Rhoda—her senses fully aroused for the first time in her life—is rapidly losing the comfort of her brash certainties. Now openly drawn to Everard, she is gripped by anxiety at the thought of yielding to desire. Insecurity and trepidation become her daily companions.

In the end, however many words are spilled between them, Everard is undone by the need to master, and Rhoda by the humiliation of self-doubt. He retreats into a conventional marriage, and she achieves a sexless independence. For one brief moment only, a small part of each of these people had reached out to embrace the difficulty of struggling toward the integrity required to form a "new" alliance—and had then fallen back to that place in the spirit where it is acceptable to no longer go on making the effort.

Following Rhoda Nunn as her polemics flare and her emotions terrify, we see that she could never have managed the consequences that the conflict between her and Barfoot have set in motion. It is her confusion that makes her so real. Hardy's Sue

Bridehead, James's Isabel Archer, Meredith's Diana of the Crossways, are all magnificent creatures—and all similarly confused, if you will—but it is in Rhoda that I see myself and others of my generation, plain. No other writer has captured the progress of our smarts, our anxieties, our bravado, as exactly as has Gissing by putting Rhoda Nunn through some very recognizable paces. Imagine (as I can all too readily) the ignorance behind that cold passion with which she, having seen the feminist light, so proudly pronounces, No equality in love? I'll do without! Children and motherhood? Unnecessary! Social castigation? Nonsense! Between the ardor of Rhoda's rhetoric and the dictates of flesh-and-blood reality lies a no-man's-land of untested conviction. How easy it was—for us as well as Rhoda—to call out angrily, To hell with all that! How chastening to experience the uncontrollable force of feeling that steadily undermines these defiant simplicities. As Rhoda moves inexorably toward the moment when she fails herself, she becomes a walking embodiment of the gap between theory and practice: the place in which so many of us have found ourselves, time and again.

Sometimes I think that for me the gap has become a deep divide at the bottom of which I wander, as though on a pilgrim's progress, still hoping to climb its side to level ground before I die.

•

A church in my neighborhood runs a soup kitchen. Every morning a line of men (I never see women on the line) stretches from the church door to the end of the block and around the corner. So many of these men are barely standing on their feet—this morning I saw one with an eye half out of its socket, another partly naked under a raincoat too tight to button—yet invariably they speak quietly among themselves, exchange newspapers, honor one another's places on the line if one drops out for a moment, all the while glancing with such patience in their eyes toward the open church door.

In the mid-1930s, a journalist named Orville John covered a fruit pickers' strike in the Imperial Valley in California and was so moved by the dignity of the strikers that he wrote of them as men bearing "ruined faces worthy of Michelangelo." Today the line outside the church brought that memorable phrase floating back into my head.

•

Last night at dinner I was telling Leonard that I'd just seen an early-thirties movie in which the leading lady plays an aviatrix (that's what she's called, an aviatrix) with whom a wealthy businessman falls desperately in love. Her spirit, her courage, her passion for flying: all undo him. At first, the pilot is in heaven: she's going to have it all; but no sooner are she and her lover married than he demands that she stop flying. Now that she's his wife, she's too valuable to risk. It develops that for the businessman, the wife's ability to pilot a plane had been the equivalent of good looks in other women: an advantageous card she held in every woman's competition to attract a worthy husband and protector. Now that *that* had been accomplished, there was no further need for her to go on flying.

Made before the code of decency took effect, the movie was wonderfully written—that is, the script was grown-up—and acted with just the right amount of grit, glamour, and pain. How come, I ask Leonard, now that we're forty years into liberationist politics we can't come up with anything nearly as artful as this? There isn't a movie, play, or novel with dialogue as good as this about the way we live now.

"That's simple," Leonard says. "Once the conflict goes public, politics thrives and art goes south. People like us are left staring at an Internet post of a raised fist, a pink ribbon, a 'right on' tattoo."

•

My mother received her invitation to the annual benefactors' luncheon at the Philharmonic and

asked me to come along as her guest. Her atten-
dance at this luncheon is a family joke.

When she had passed the thirty-year mark as a
subscriber to the Philharmonic's Friday afternoon
concerts, she—who lived on Social Security and a
tiny union pension—was invited out to lunch by the
orchestra's PR man. She thought she was being
thanked for having been a loyal music lover, but as
it turned out she was being wooed as a potential
donor who would remember the Philharmonic in
her will. When she realized what was up, she said,
"Oh, it's my *money* you're after! Okay, I'll leave you
two hundred."

The PR man, accustomed to being left thousands, blinked at her. "Two *hundred*?" he echoed in
disbelief.

"All right," she replied disgustedly, "five hundred."

Seemingly at the same moment, each realized
the magnitude of the misunderstanding and both
began to guffaw. On the spot, the PR man made my
mother a Friend of the Philharmonic and she had
received an invitation to the annual benefactors'
luncheon ever since.

In the dining room at Lincoln Center, the pre-
sentation is already under way. This same PR man
stands before a blackboard covered with numbers;
he has a pointer in his hand and is speaking to the

room at large. At small round tables sit men and women in blue suits and silk dresses, nonetheless looking very much like my mother, who is dressed in polyester. Age is the great leveler here.

My mother sits down in an empty seat, pulls me into the one beside her, and signals the waiter imperiously for her chicken salad.

"And after your death," the man at the blackboard is saying, "the Philharmonic can get this money you've bestowed on it with these tax breaks I'm now outlining. If you choose plan B, your children may complain that under this plan they'll be losing forty thousand dollars in IRS costs. But"— he smiles broadly at the company—"you can take care of that complaint easily. Just take out an insurance policy, and *leave* them an extra forty thousand."

My mother looks at me in open amusement; then she snorts, then laughs out loud as the PR man goes on giving instructions on how to leave a clear hundred thousand to the famous orchestra. People turn to look at her, but no matter, she's enjoying herself hugely. I've learned to stay calm at these moments.

The meal over, she rises quickly and hustles onto the reception line filing past the PR man, whose hand everyone wants to shake. When he sees her, he grasps her hand and calls out, "Hello! How are *you*?"

"Do you know who I am?" she asks coyly.

"Indeed I do," comes the hearty reply.

She stands there beaming. He knows who she is. She's the woman who's beat the system. She has no money, yet here she is, keeping a gimlet eye on the hoi polloi as they sprinkle some of their ill-gotten gains on culture. It is the high point of the morning, the triumph of the day; after this, all is anticlimax. I tried hard to make my mother a feminist, but this morning I see that for her, nothing in this life will trump class. No matter. In the vitalizing end, one is as good as the other.

•

On a rainy afternoon in midweek I purchase a ticket for a Broadway revival of *Gypsy*. Inflation being what it is, I'm still sitting in the balcony. No matter. From the second the score comes surging out of the pit and I hear again its romantic antiromantic sound—the sound, as Leonard used to say, of every musical that was never written—I begin to melt into the delicious warmth of nostalgia, preparing myself for a good wallow. To my surprise I find the pleasure slow in coming, and as the show goes on, something like withdrawal pains begins replacing the expectation of pleasure. I seem to have forgotten how raw *Gypsy* is, how visceral its resentments and unrelenting its bitter drumbeat. On second

thought, perhaps it's not that I've forgotten; perhaps it is rather that I'm no longer the audience for
this piece of theater I've always regarded as iconic.

The first time I saw *Gypsy* I was in my twenties
and Ethel Merman was playing Rose, the most in-
famous stage mother on record. Merman was one of
the great belters of our time, with an acting style to
match. In her performance there was no shading,
no nuance, no second thoughts. She was a natural
force onstage—crude and overwhelming—and I
loved it. I loved it with a hard, pressing love that
frightened and exhilarated me. The shocking, gutsy,
no-holds-barred sound of that vulgar insistence,
the sheer drive of it! I knew it well. I'd grown up
with it. Rose was a monster—Leonard calls her the
Jewish Hedda Gabler—I could see that, anyone
could see that: fierce, ignorant, hungry. Yes, yes, yes.
Here I was, this college girl barely out of the immigrant ghetto, with a sense of the world belonging to
everyone but me, and I'm suffocating on an energy
that comes from so far down inside it makes its
own laws; provides me with a sense of nature denied that could urge an anarchist to throw a bomb.
When "Rose's Turn" reached the balcony, my head
was bursting with a joy of recognition that nothing
could diminish or ever make seem unjustified. Rose
was a monster? So what. She was *my* monster. She
was up there doing it for me. Years later I sat in a

movie theater, watching some black exploitation movie, and as the protagonist on the screen mowed down everyone in sight, and I heard everyone around me scream, "Yes! Yes! Yes!" I understood in my bones the murderous glee of the audience. After all, I'd seen Ethel Merman mowing them down and felt the same.

The brilliance of *Gypsy*—the story of a celebrated stripper and her outrageous mother—lies in its point of view. It is a point of view that makes you hear Jule Styne's music "twice," delighting the first time around in the childish cynicism of "Let Me Entertain You," cringing the second time at its shocking contempt.

Rose moves forward blindly, alienating everyone with the speed and power of her need, at the same time dragging them along behind her. No one—including herself—is real to her, yet each goodbye is an intolerable loss. Toward the end, when even the devoted Herbie is finally leaving her, Rose is so confused she cries out, "You're jealous, like every other man I've ever known. Because my girls come first!" This at the moment when she is about to push her daughter Louise onto a burlesque stage, hissing at her, "You'll promise them everything, and give them nothing." Within seconds Louise will become the Gypsy Rose Lee who comes out onstage announcing, "My mother got me into this business. She said,

'Promise them everything and give them nothing.'"
Then she looks mockingly at the deranged men sal-
ivating in front of her, and tells them, "But I'll give
you everything. Only you have to beg." Before our
eyes an even greater monster is born.

The moment is stark. We see what the play has
been driving toward all along: the human fallout of
Rose's deracinated hunger.

Now, decades later, I look around me when
Gypsy reaches "Rose's Turn." There are so many
young faces (black as well as white, boys as well
as girls) looking as my own had once looked: eyes
shining, mouths open, screaming, "Yes, yes, yes!"
I feel my own face congealing as theirs grow ever
more mobile, and I find myself thinking, There's
no way around this one, there is only the going
through it.

It's the gene for anarchy, alive in everyone born
into the wrong class, the wrong color, the wrong
sex—only in some it stays quiescent, while in some
it makes a holocaust—no one knows this better
than me.

In the 1970s, at a time when social unhappiness
seemed to be erupting all over the United States,
and thousands in America were adopting the speech
and tactics of antisocial rebellion, I joined in the
raging intemperateness of exploding radical feminism: "Marriage is an institution of oppression!"

"Love is rape!" "Sleeping with the enemy!" When I think back on it, I realize that we, the feminists of the seventies and eighties, had become primitive anarchists. We didn't want reform, we didn't even want reparations; what we wanted was to bring down the system, destroy the social arrangement, no matter the consequence. When asked (as we were, repeatedly) "What about the children? What about the family?" we snarled (or roared), "Fuck the children! Fuck the family! This is the moment to declare our grievance, and make others feel it as we do. What comes later is not our concern."

Here we were, women of the law-abiding middle class sounding, at this crucial moment of unmediated revolt, like professional insurrectionists, when in reality we were just Rose, demanding our turn.

Watching *Gypsy*, the word *just* leaves me with the taste of ashes in my mouth.

·

The other day I thought I saw Johnny Dylan sitting on a bench in Madison Square Park. Impossible, of course, as he's dead, but the moment was so vivid that it put me instantly in mind of what in my life he had come to signify.

Ten or fifteen years ago, we were forever running into each other somewhere in the neighborhood—either on Greenwich Avenue, or in Sheridan Square, or at the corner of Fifth and Fourteenth— and when we did we'd both come to an instant halt. I'd say hello, he'd bob his head, and for a moment we'd stand there beaming at each other. After that I'd say, "How are ya?" and wait calmly while Johnny's voice struggled to find a register in which, one by one, the syllables could free themselves to become words no longer strangling in his throat.

It was John Dylan who taught me how to wait. He was in his sixties then, smaller and much thinner than he'd once been, but his blue eyes were lit with a beautiful kind of gravity and his narrow face imprinted with the wisdom of inflicted patience. Sometimes the quiet trapped in that patience seemed immense, and it would flash through me how much more alone he was than even the rest of us.

He had had a stroke that had left him aphasic and had effectively ended one of the most impressive acting careers in the New York theater. In the eighties and nineties, the Public Theater had been his territory and Beckett monologues his signature work. Doleful and magisterial, it had been the work of a man in superb control of the material. After the stroke, John pulled himself back from the dead through an act of disciplined will that spoke directly to how art—both in spirit and in body— really gets made; but no one thought ever again to hear the great Irish playwright's words emerging from that twisted mouth.

Johnny had lived for years in Westbeth, the Bell Laboratories building in the Village that had been converted in 1970 into subsidized artists' housing. The place takes up a square block, its backside facing the West Side Highway and the Hudson River— John's studio apartment had a river view—and it contains a population of painters, dancers, and writers, many of whom would have been on welfare times without number if not for the low Westbeth rent.

I've always thought those river apartments reflect the alternating surges of promise and desolation that the building itself seems to induce. On a Saturday night in spring, with the current moving swiftly in the open windows, boats outlined in lights, high-rises glowing across the water, laughter in the hallways beyond the studio door, these rooms are infused with a sense of New York everlasting; then again, on a Sunday afternoon in winter, with the river gray and frozen, not a human being in sight, and the city an abstraction, the same space fills up with an overpowering solitariness that seems to echo through what now feels like miles of vacant corridors on the other side of the door.

One day a few years before he died, I received an invitation to a seven o'clock reading by John Dylan to be held in his Westbeth studio apartment. What on earth? I thought, and went. When I arrived I found twenty or thirty people sitting on folding chairs lined up in rows, facing the river. At a space between the windows stood a round wooden table and a chair; on the table, a gooseneck lamp and a sheaf of manuscript. I found a seat in a middle row, one in from the book-lined wall to my right.

At seven o'clock Johnny came forward and sat down in the chair between the windows. He placed his hands on the manuscript and looked out at us for a moment. The room went dark except for the pool of light shining down on the table, and John began to read from Beckett's monologue *Texts for Nothing*. His voice—unlike the voice I usually heard on the street—was now remarkably steady and did not sound at all like the voice of an actor reading. It sounded, instead, like that of a man speaking directly from the heart.

"Suddenly, no, at last, long last," John said quietly, "I couldn't any more, I couldn't go on. Someone said, You can't stay here. I couldn't stay there and I couldn't go on . . . How can I go on . . . It's simple, I can do nothing any more, that's what you think. I say to the body, Up with you now, and I can feel it struggling, struggling no more, struggling again, till it gives up. I say to the head, Leave it alone, stay quiet, it stops breathing, then pants on worse than ever . . . I should turn away from it all, away from the body, away from the head, let them work it out between them, let them cease, I can't, it's I would have to cease. Ah yes, we seem to be more than one, all deaf, gathered together for life."

We all sat up straighter in our folding chairs, and the many little movements of an audience not yet engaged came to an abrupt halt. Into the expanded silence John spoke again, but, abruptly, his strong start began to lose momentum, and the instability that haunts his speech came creeping back. His voice began to go up when it should have gone down, to crack when it should have stayed firm, rush forward when it should have held back. Yet, surprisingly, on this night the unreliability did not jar, and the performance remained absorbing. Slowly, I realized that this was because John wasn't fighting the loss of control. It was as if he had known it would be coming and had figured out a survival tactic in advance. He would go with it, ride it, in fact make use of wherever it landed him.

"How long have I been he-e-e-ere?" he screeched when I was certain the script called for dullness of tone—and the screech felt right.

"What-a-question," he rushed on. "An-hour-a-month-a-year-a-century, depending on what I meant by here, and me, and being and there"—and the speed became exciting.

Repeatedly, he moved into the skid. Wherever his voice wanted to go, he let it go; whatever it wished to do, he let it do. And Beckett accommodated him. Beckett's words danced, climbed, crawled, to make the sense that Johnny's voice needed to make of them, and the work remained compelling. Starting, stopping, jerking about, starting up again, the piece began to sound as if it had been written for this very reading.

Then a man in a seat near the wall reached out toward the bookcases and turned a switch on a tape machine. Suddenly, John's voice of twenty years earlier, reading the same monologue, flooded the room. That mannered vibrancy—the unmistakable sound of "Beckett acting" in full command of itself—washed over the company.

"I've given myself up for dead all over the place," the forty-year-old John intoned with magisterial dolefulness, "of hunger, of old age, murdered, drowned, and then for no reason, of tedium, nothing like breathing your last to put new life in you . . ." The voice on the tape paused, and we did not doubt that "pause" was written in the script. "Above is the light," it went on, "the elements, a kind of light, sufficient to see by, the living find their ways . . ." It paused again and confided elegantly, "To have suffered under that miserable light, what a blunder."

At the table between the windows, above the pool of lamplight, John's face glistened with sweat. The tape machine switched off, and in a strangled whisper the man at the table spat out, "And if I went back to where all went out and on from there, no, that would lead nowhere, never led anywhere, I tried throwing me off a cliff, collapsing in the street, in the midst of mortals, that led nowhere, I gave up . . . Dribble on here till time is done, murmuring every ten centuries, It's not me, it's not true, it's not me, I'm far . . . Quick, quick before I weep."

The tape switched back on.

"I don't know," the intact John observed. "I'm here, that's all I know, and that it's still not me, it's of that the best has to be made . . . Leave all that, to want to leave all that, not knowing, what that means, all that."

The machine went off.

"Where would I go," the man at the table croaked, his face now bathed in sweat. "If I could go, who would I be, if I could be, what would I say, if I had a voice, who says this, saying it's me?" He stopped. "It's not me . . ." Stopped again. "It's not me . . . what a thought . . . There is only me, this evening, here on earth, and a voice that makes no sound because it goes towards none." Stop. "No need of a story, a story is not compulsory, just a life, that's the mistake I made, one of the mistakes, to have wanted a story for myself, whereas life alone is enough." Stop. "I'm making progress." Stop. "I am here." Stop. "I stay here, sitting, if I'm sitting, often I feel sitting, sometimes standing, it's one or the other, or lying down, there's another possibility, often I feel lying down, it's one of the three, or kneeling." Stop.

"What counts is to be in the world, the posture is immaterial, so long as one is on earth. To breathe is all that is required." Stop. "Yes, there are moments, like this moment, when I seem almost restored to the feasible. Then it goes, all goes, and I'm far again . . . I wait for me afar for my story to begin."

And so on to the end, the dramatic, knowing voice of the forty-year-old John Dylan continually up against the cracked, exalted one of the Dylan who by now had lived Beckett's script.

Outside, the river ran dark and turbulent; across the water, banks of high-rise light shot into the sky; in the hall beyond the studio door, three people were having a neighborly argument. The water, the lights, the words in the hallway: all seemed to group themselves around the small, drained figure bowing in front of the wooden table without touching it. The figure itself remained gloriously solitary: beyond pain, pleasure, or threat. I knew that I had been hearing Beckett—really hearing him—for the first time.

•

It was a cold, clear morning in March. Having just
finished interviewing a city official for a piece I was
writing, I was sitting at the counter of a coffee shop
across the street from City Hall, drinking coffee,
eating a bagel, and writing down remembered
snatches of the conversation I'd just had when a
man sat down one stool away from me. He wore
dark pants and a tweed jacket, looked to be in his
fifties, and I took him to be a middle-rank civil ser-
vant. When I had finished eating, drinking, and
writing, I stood up, and as I was gathering myself
together, he said to me, "I hope you won't mind, I
haven't been able to read a word you're writing, but
I'd like to tell you some things I know about you
from your handwriting." Startled, I said, "Sure, go
ahead." I took a better look at him then and saw
that he wore a large Native American turquoise-
and-silver ring and a string tie. He leaned toward
me and said slowly but intently, "You're generous.
That is, you are inclined to be generous, but circumstances don't allow you to be. So you're often not.
You're assertive. And a bit aggressive. And that
small script . . . you're very literate, very intelligent." I stared at him for a fraction of a second.
"Thanks," I said. "That's a fine flattering portrait
you've drawn." He looked relieved that I wasn't

somehow offended. Then I said, "Is my handwriting really so small?" He nodded and said yes, it was, and small handwriting, he repeated, is the mark of the very intelligent. Of course, he added (very softly), there are people who have much smaller handwriting, and they . . . "Are the mad or the brilliant," I said, finishing his sentence for him. He paused. "Yes," he said, again softly, "they're often very brilliant." I stood there, looking steadily, perhaps even gravely, at him. He smiled and said, "Oh, don't worry, my handwriting is twice as large as yours." I *did* burst out laughing then, but the remark kept crawling around under my skin for the whole rest of that day.

•

It's an evening in June and I am taking a turn through Washington Square. As I stroll, I see in the air before me, like an image behind a scrim, the square as it looked when I was young, standing right behind the square that I'm actually looking at. That was a good fifty years ago, when my friends and I used to come down from the Bronx and in from Brooklyn on summer evenings and we'd walk around looking at a piece of world so different from that of our own neighborhoods we might as well have been in Europe. The square was pristine then—paths swept clean, benches freshly painted,

fountain sparkling—and the verdancy a marvel:
thousands of leaves glistening on the century-old
trees, every bush and flower bed neatly trimmed,
the grass green velvet. And the people in the square!
It was middle-class bohemia then, the women sensual, the men poetic, and of course everyone white.
To our hungry young eyes the scene promised culture and class privilege . . . not a thought in our
heads then about race or sex . . . we couldn't wait
to get there. Romantic longing washed through all of
us for years, and we were haunted by the beauty of
the square on those sweet summer evenings.

Now, here it is another summer evening and
I am again walking in the square. With the street at
my back and everything I know etched on my face,
I look through the scrim directly into those old
memories and I see that they no longer have author-
ity over me. I see the square as it is—black, brown,
young; swarming with drifters and junkies and
lousy guitar players—and I feel myself as I am, the
city as it is. I have lived out my conflicts not my fantasies, and so has New York. We are at one.

•

On the other side of the square I run into Leonard,
serendipitously out for his own stroll this evening. I
start to tell him what I've been remembering, but he
is nodding before I'm through a dozen sentences.

He understands almost by osmosis what I am saying because he was there himself, all those years ago, on those same summer evenings. "We were probably both trying to pick up the same guys," he laughs. Then he says, "But I, too, was lusting after the couples. Trying desperately to talk myself into 'normal.' What were we? Sixteen? Seventeen? Somehow, even then, I knew I'd never make it. Never."

We walk on together, side by side; silent; mirror-image witnesses, each of us, to the other's formative experience. The exchange will always deepen, even if the friendship does not.

·

It is now October. On a Saturday evening in mid-month, Daniel takes me down to the Winter Garden in Battery Park City to hear a group of Renaissance singers in concert. I have many times walked through this lovely open hall with its marble floors and great central staircase, the glittering shops and restaurants, and the tall arched window filled with New York Harbor. Who could have imagined that this elaborate piece of architectural commerce and kitsch would become such a New York treat? But it has, filling up at all hours with people streaming through to shop, eat, wander, listen to the free music and theater pieces presented most days at noon or in the evening at seven or eight.

We come early to secure seats close to the movable stage set up before the arched window, then wander off, buy sandwiches and coffee, sit beside the water. The evening is soft, with the harbor and promenade gleaming under the strung lights of boats and restaurant terraces, the atmosphere festive, sparkling, somehow (lovely word!) expectant. When we return to our seats darkness has fallen, and the great hall is buzzing with humanity. I look about me, and to my amazement the entire staircase, receding stadium-like, up the back of the hall, rising four or five stories high, is packed. Turning back in my seat, I feel a thrill shoot through my body, the kind that occurs when a nerve is touched. A thousand people are gathered here, grouped all over the hall, waiting to feel themselves in the music.

For the first time in decades, I feel the spirit of Lewisohn Stadium alive at my back, and I think, I'm always being told you people have left the city in droves, but look, you're still here. Oh, you've shifted positions, to be sure, you don't dominate the scene anymore, the city is no longer made in your image, but here you are; and here am I; and there are the singers. It takes all of us together to fill the hall with joy and, urban death or no urban death, the city is still up for it.

•

A friend reads what I've been writing and says to me over coffee, "You're romanticizing the street. Don't you know that New York has lost seventy-five percent of its manufacturing base?" In my mind's eye, I stare into the faces of all the women and men with whom I interact daily. Hey, you people, I address them silently, did you hear what my friend just said? The city is doomed, the middle class has deserted New York, the corporations are in Texas, Jersey, Taiwan. You're gone, you're outta here, it's all over. How come you're still on the street?

New York isn't jobs, they reply, it's temperament. Most people are in New York because they need evidence—in large quantities—of human expressiveness; and they need it not now and then, but every day. That is what they *need*. Those who go off to the manageable cities can do without; those who come to New York cannot.

Or perhaps I should say that it is I who cannot.

•

It's the voices I can't do without. In most cities of the world the populace is planted in centuries of cobblestoned alleys, ruined churches, architectural relics, none of which are ever dug up, only piled one on top of another. If you've grown up in New York, your life is an archaeology not of structures but of voices, also piled one on top of another, also not really replacing one another:

On Sixth Avenue, two small, dark-skinned men lean against a parked cab. One says to the other, "Look, it's very simple. A is the variable costs, B is the gross income, C is the overhead. Got that?" The other man shakes his head no. "Dummy!" the first man cries. "You gotta *get* it."

On Park Avenue, a well-dressed matron says to her friend, "When I was young, men were the main course, now they're a condiment."

On Fifty-Seventh Street, one boyish-looking man says to another, "I didn't realize you were such good friends. What did she give you, that you miss her so?" "It wasn't what she gave me," the other replies, "it was what she didn't take away."

As the cabbie on Sixth Avenue says, someone's gotta get it; and late in the day, someone does.

I am walking on Eighth Avenue during the five o'clock rush, thinking of changing a word in a sentence, and somewhere in the Forties, I don't notice the light turning red. Halfway into the path of an oncoming truck, I am lifted off my feet by a pair of hands on my upper arms and pulled back onto the curb. The hands do not release me immediately. I am pressed to the chest of the person to whom the hands belong. I can still feel the beating heart against my back. When I turn to thank my rescuer

I am looking into the middle-aged face of an over-weight man with bright blue eyes, straw-colored hair, and a beet-red face. We stare wordlessly at each other. I'll never know what the man is thinking at this moment, but the expression on his face is un-forgettable. Me, I am merely shaken, but he looks as though transfigured by what has just happened. His eyes are fixed on mine, but I see that they are really looking inward. I realize that this is *his* experience, not mine. It is he who has felt the urgency of life—he is still holding it in his hands.

Two hours later I am home, having dinner at my table, looking out at the city. My mind flashes on all who crossed my path today. I hear their voices, I see their gestures, I start filling in lives for them. Soon they are company, great company. I think to myself, I'd rather be here with you tonight than with anyone else I know. Well, almost anyone else I know. I look up at the great clock on my wall, the one that gives the date as well as the hour. It's time to call Leonard.